REMEMBERING THE BATTLE OF THE CRATER

REMEMBERING THE BATTLE OF
THE CRATER

War as Murder

KEVIN M. LEVIN

UNIVERSITY PRESS OF KENTUCKY

Editorial and Sales Offices: The University Press of Kentucky
663 South Limestone Street, Lexington, Kentucky 40508–4008

ISBN 978-0-8131-3610-3

Manufactured in the United States of America.

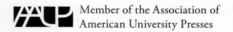 Member of the Association of
American University Presses

Book Club Edition

For Ela

CONTENTS

ILLUSTRATIONS

INTRODUCTION

IN DECEMBER 2003 moviegoers were treated to a vivid re-creation of the battle of the Crater in the movie *Cold Mountain,* directed by Anthony Minghella. Though the battle, which was fought just outside Petersburg, Virginia, on July 30, 1864, was not included in the original work of fiction by Charles Frazier, it was used in the film as a dramatic opening to set the stage for Inman (played by Jude Law) and his decision to leave the Confederate army and head back to his lover (played by Nicole Kidman), still living in western North Carolina and working desperately to make ends meet. The opening sequence presents the important stages of the battle, including the initial massive detonation of explosives under a Confederate salient, the advance of Federal soldiers into the crater, and the hand-to-hand combat that left thousands dead and wounded, resulting ultimately in a decisive victory for General Robert E. Lee's Army of Northern Virginia.

The movie accurately portrayed the bloody fighting in and around the crater and probably satisfied the demands of most Civil War enthusiasts. The movie also briefly acknowledged the presence of United States Colored Troops (USCTs). At one point in the battle sequence, a black Union soldier and a Native American in Confederate uniform exchange glances. Minghella's negotiation of the race issue, however, avoids any references to the well-documented executions of many black soldiers after their surrender.

Minghella's historic representation of the battle of the Crater takes its place in the long and complex history of race and Civil War memory stretching back to the accounts that the soldiers themselves wrote after the battle.

1

If we step back, however, it is impossible not to acknowledge the wide gulf, with regard to race, between the accounts the soldiers wrote and the way subsequent generations remembered and commemorated the event, from the nineteenth century up to the eve of the Civil War sesquicentennial.

It is the absence of race, exemplified here in *Cold Mountain,* that is the subject of this book: this process of preserving a certain kind of memory that moves to minimize or ignore the participation of USCTs in one of the bloodiest battles of the Civil War. Understanding how memory of this racial component was shaped at various points during the 150 years since the end of the war allows us the opportunity to peer into the changes and challenges experienced by the nation at large. More important, the study of memory allows us to understand the extent to which previous interpretations of the past were subject to political, social, and economic pressures, and how difficult it was for individuals and communities outside of dominant power structures to preserve and commemorate their preferred understanding of the past.

This book has benefited from the vast amount of research that has been done over the past few decades on the Civil War and historical memory. It is not surprising that historians have embraced the study of Civil War memory. The Civil War is ideally suited to an examination of the cultural, social, and political shifts that have shaped our understanding of this nation's defining moment. One does not need to look far for evidence of the competing claims on history made by different social groups active in the decades following the war. From research on the influences of the Lost Cause to the role of national reconciliation to the examination of individual battles, monument dedications, textbooks, children's literature, and commemorative rituals, the focus on memory has aided in uncovering the fluid cultural, political, and racial factors that, in large part, determined whose understanding of the past became legitimized and integral to the formation and maintenance of an evolving national identity.[1]

In many ways this book builds on the scholarship of David Blight, whose book *Race and Reunion* introduced a readership to the subject of historical memory, a subject extending beyond the narrow confines of the academy. In Blight's view, the veterans on both sides of the Potomac chose to assign the deepest meaning of the war to the heroism and valor of the soldiers on the battlefield. The shared experiences of soldierhood was a theme that could bring former enemies together peacefully on old battlefields. Forging bonds of valor between onetime enemies, however, required that questions surrounding emancipation and race be ignored. According to Blight, the success of national reconciliation and reunion over the "emancipationist legacy" guaranteed that the role of African Americans in the Civil War would be minimized to the point of nonrecognition.[2]

Readers will find elements of Blight's thesis throughout this book, but my analysis of memory at the Crater will reveal places where his examination of the multiple traditions that came out of the Civil War does not go far enough in explaining the interplay of race and politics in national reconciliation as well as the deep divisions between former Confederates and white Virginians. Confederates who fought in the Virginia brigade at the Crater were united in their defense of Petersburg from black Union soldiers. This was the first time that Lee's men were forced to fight former slaves, and the rage they felt—which led to the well-documented slaughter of captured black soldiers after the battle—reflected, like nothing else could, just what was at stake in the event of Confederate defeat. Confederates' experience at the Crater, including their participation in one of the final decisive victories in Virginia, served as a foundation for reunions among the veterans of the brigade in the 1870s on the old battlefield. However, these continued bonds of affection were not immune from the political disputes connected to Virginia's fragile postwar racial hierarchy.[3]

The most contentious point centered on former major general William Mahone, who led the Confederate counterattack and was widely credited for saving the Army of Northern Virginia and Petersburg. Mahone used the fame that went along with a successful military career to further his own postwar projects, first as a railroad magnate and later as a politician. By 1883, Mahone had become one of the most controversial and divisive politicians in the country. As the organizer and leader of the Readjuster Party (named for its policy of downwardly "readjusting" Virginia's state debt), Mahone led a highly successful independent coalition of black and white Republicans and white Democrats. Readjusters governed the state from 1879 to 1883, electing a governor and two U.S. senators, and they served in six of Virginia's ten congressional districts. Their legislative agenda and Mahone's prominent role within the party and in the U.S. Senate generated heated attacks in newspapers as well as in more personal forms of communication.

As had former Confederate general James Longstreet, Mahone incurred the wrath of a growing "Lost Cause" movement that, in addition to rationalizing Confederate defeat, sought to maintain Democratic Party solidarity by fostering white supremacy and states' rights. Lost Cause advocates such as Jubal Early assumed an aggressive posture against ex-Confederates like Mahone who threatened their own conservative social and political agenda. As Mahone was not an outsider but a successful Confederate general, he had to be dealt with severely, and they dealt with him by attacking his war record, including his leadership at the battle of the Crater. A closer look at Mahone's postwar difficulties sheds light on the heated debates surrounding the limits to which the Confederate past could be used to serve current political ends, and in doing so it undermines the notion that "Virginia history" and "Confederate history" became nearly synonymous in the first few decades after the war.

The Crater also hosted numerous reunions between former enemies. Veterans praised one another for their bravery and reflected on their shared values as Americans. They accomplished this by suppressing their bitter memories of the black soldiers or by sharing their remembered outrage in public forums in a way that conformed to the current political and racial atmosphere. Reunions even led to the possibility of early preservation of the Crater battlefield through its purchase by Northern investors. This was not to be, however. A closer look at the Crater, though, reveals the limits of sectional reunion. Virginians exercised a great deal of control over how the battlefield was remembered and they did so in the form of two major reenactments, one in 1903 and one in 1937, that highlighted the local and regional veterans who had served in Mahone's Virginia brigade.[4]

The strong pull of reconciliation is also inadequate to explain the relatively late inclusion of some sections of the Petersburg battlefield in the National Military Park system compared to the first five battlefield parks, which were organized in the 1880s and 1890s. Unlike other major battlefields, the earthworks around Petersburg could not be contained within an easily defined park boundary. Because there was no boundary between the earthworks and the rest of the city, the battlefield was often seen as an obstacle to continued economic expansion, especially during times of economic depression. As a result, few area residents placed the need to preserve sacred ground above commercial development. This was most clearly the case in the development of an eighteen-hole golf course on the Crater battlefield during the 1920s.[5]

During the first two decades after the war, Petersburg's African American community publicly commemorated its military heritage, most notably through its local Virginia militia. Public speakers acknowledged the bravery of black Union soldiers and the need to maintain their collective memory as part of a broader story of emancipation and freedom. Outside Petersburg, a small number of black writers and former USCT officers penned accounts that not only preserved an important aspect of Civil War history but acknowledged the bravery of the men in the ranks at a time when the fruits of the freedom they had helped to secure were gradually deteriorating because of the resurgence of "Redeemer" governments in the South and a national memory of the war largely structured around reconciliation. This black narrative of the war, featuring USCTs and the battlefields on which they fought, would eventually blossom into a full-blown counter-memory that worked to highlight the continued racial injustices of the 1950s and 1960s as white Americans commemorated the Civil War centennial.[6]

It was not until the Civil War centennial celebrations of the 1960s and the concurrent civil rights movement that African Americans were able to challenge both white political control of local and national government and a predominantly white memory of the war, infused with elements of the Lost Cause and reconciliation. The political inroads made by African Americans in the 1970s and beyond have inevitably led to substantial changes in the way public spaces such as battlefields are used to commemorate the past.

The current debate surrounding battlefield interpretation is part of a much larger transformation that is taking place predominantly in the South. As the region continues to be transformed by the active political participation of African Americans and other minorities, there has been a push for its public spaces, including Civil War battlefields, to reflect more closely a broader and more diverse past. This can be clearly seen in Petersburg itself, as the city and National Park Service explore opportunities to break down some of the barriers that have prevented the black community from identifying with the history of these landscapes. The challenges the nation faces as it enters the Civil War sesquicentennial revolve around the question of how to remember the most divisive event from its past. However, before we look forward, it would be wise to look back.

Chapter 1

THE BATTLE

"Until Every Negro Has Been Slaughtered"

THE PRISONERS WERE placed in formation, in lines four abreast. Officers led the way, followed by alternating ranks of four black and four white soldiers. The column was ordered to parade through the streets of Petersburg in full view of the town's remaining civilian population. The roughly 1,500 black and white Union prisoners, who had been captured the day before, July 30, 1864, after their failed assault, were being used to send a strong message: to the men serving in Robert E. Lee's Army of Northern Virginia, to the remaining white residents of Petersburg, and to the Confederacy as a whole. As the prisoners marched and countermarched through the streets, they were subjected to taunts and verbal abuses from spectators at the street level and on verandas, which offered perhaps the best view of this unusual scene. Lieutenant Freeman S. Bowley recalled years later that once the column entered the city, "we were assailed by a volley of abuse from men, women and children that exceeded anything of the kind that I ever heard." The cries of "See the white and nigger equality soldiers" and "Yanks and niggers sleep in the same bed!" suggest that the intended message of this interracial march of prisoners had come through loud and clear, accomplishing all it had set out to do and more.[1]

The order to march both black and white Union prisoners through Petersburg served to remind soldiers and civilians alike of just what was at stake as the American Civil War entered its fourth summer. The torrents of abuse hurled that early Sunday morning were directed first and foremost at the black Union soldiers (now stripped of their uniforms), some of whom were once the property of Virginia slave owners. Their presence on the battlefield reinforced horrific fears of miscegenation, the raping of white Southern women, and black political control that had surfaced at various times throughout the antebellum period and that many had come to believe would ensue if victory were not secured.

The fear that animated the black soldiers as they endured the taunts of their captors and the sting of public humiliation was of a different sort. For these men the recent fight had been an opportunity to finally prove themselves on the field of battle and impress upon both their white officers and the rest of the nation that they were worthy of respect as men, as soldiers and, potentially, as future citizens of a nation reborn out of the ashes of slavery. Now, as they marched through the city, they couldn't be certain that they would escape the fate of their black comrades who had been executed in the immediate wake of the battle. In addition to the bursts of rage exhibited on the streets by a restless public, black soldiers also had to cope with resentment and anger from many of their fellow white soldiers, who felt humiliated at having to march in formation with them rather than in their normal segregated units, as well as from their own white officers, some of whom chose to lie about their unit identification.[2]

Once the parade ended, the men were marched to Merchant Island, situated in the Appomattox River, where they awaited transportation to prisons in Richmond and Danville, Virginia, or Salisbury, North Carolina. Some black soldiers fared much worse. Confederate authorities refused to treat them as prisoners and instead allowed area slave owners to review them in hopes of locating and reclaiming fugitive slaves.[3]

Accounts of what eventually came to be known as the battle of the Crater or Mine tend to ignore or downplay this moment in the overall narrative of the battle. Instead, historians and other writers have tended to focus on the construction of the mine shaft, the early morning massive detonation of 8,000 pounds of explosives that ripped through a Confederate brigade, and the fierce battle that ensued—all of which fits into the scale of violence that had developed by the summer of 1864. On the other hand, the failure to adequately account for the presence of an entire division of United States Colored Troops and what its presence meant to the men who took part in this battle tells us a great deal about how our collective memory of this particular battle and the war as a whole has evolved since 1865. In ignoring this prisoner march of black and white soldiers, however, we fail to understand and appreciate a salient factor of this particular battle, one that was not and could not be ignored by those engaged.

The battle that took place on July 30, 1864, grew out of a costly campaign in Virginia that stretched from the Rappahannock River to the

Appomattox between the beginning of May and mid-June. Beginning on May 5 and continuing through the first two weeks of June, General Ulysses S. Grant's Army of the Potomac (commanded by General George G. Meade) and General Robert E. Lee's Army of Northern Virginia engaged in some of the fiercest fighting of the entire war. The two armies clashed at such places as the Wilderness, Spotsylvania Court House, the North Anna River, Cold Harbor, and along the defensive perimeter around the city of Petersburg. Although outnumbered two to one, Lee managed to stave off numerous attacks and keep his army between the Federals and the Confederate capital of Richmond. The fierce fighting that defined the Overland campaign cost both armies dearly, especially the Army of the Potomac, which lost upward of 50,000 men; although Lee's army suffered less, its 33,000 casualties constituted a higher percentage in an army numbered around 60,000.[4]

Grant had hoped to cajole Lee into a decisive battle that would decide the war in Virginia, but as his army pushed closer to Richmond, his thoughts centered on shifting the fighting south of the James River to Petersburg. Five railroad lines connected Petersburg with the rest of the Confederacy: the Richmond and Petersburg Railroad, the Southside Railroad, Weldon Railroad, the Norfolk Railroad, and the City Point Railroad. Disruption of those lifelines would not only seriously hamper Lee's operations and jeopardize Richmond but damage the overall Confederate war effort.

Beginning on June 12 the Army of the Potomac moved out from its positions around Cold Harbor. This final turning movement was led by Major General William Smith's Eighteenth Corps, which moved by ship to Bermuda Hundred while the rest of the army marched to the James River crossings. Once across, the lead elements of Grant's army were within a day's march of Petersburg. Lee's army remained in its positions, convinced that operations would resume in the vicinity of Richmond.

Smith's Eighteenth Corps, which numbered around 12,500 and included a small division of USCTs under the command of General Edward W. Hinks, reached the outer defenses of Petersburg close to noon on June 15. The defense of Petersburg was left to 2,200 old men and young boys under the command of former Virginia governor Brigadier General Henry A. Wise. Their defenses—called the "Dimmock Line" after Captain Charles H. Dimmock, who commenced construction back in the summer of 1862—consisted of a chain of massive breastworks and gun emplacements that began east of the city on the Appomattox River and ended on the river just west of the city, thus forming a semicircle. The attack on June 15 succeeded in capturing a series of strong artillery positions east of Petersburg, but Smith resisted Hinks's suggestion to continue the attack and possibly take the city itself. Major General Winfield S. Hancock's Second Corps arrived overnight while Lieutenant General Pierre G. T. Beauregard transferred units to Petersburg, which brought their numbers to around 14,000. Attacks continued during the next two days, but they failed to break Confederate defenses. Smaller operations continued in mid-June as Union forces severed two minor railroad lines east of Petersburg, but the Southside and Weldon railroads continued to supply Lee's army, which now numbered around 50,000 and occupied a line some twenty-six miles long between Richmond and Petersburg. Grant's force constituted an impressive host, hovering around 112,000 troops.[5]

The constant digging between the two armies resulted in a forward line buttressed by enclosed redans, or forts, plus additional trenches behind the forward line connected by zigzagging communication trenches. The entire system was finally connected to the rear with sunken roads and covered ways, which were vital for shifting men and supplies out of sight of enemy guns. Work was regularly conducted in conditions topping 100 degrees with no rain throughout the period between the battle of Cold Harbor and July 19. With both armies committed to the protection afforded by their earthworks, life in the trenches was reduced to a monotonous regularity.[6]

A notable exception to this pattern materialized during the final week of June in the center of the Union position, where the two armies were situated barely 100 yards from one another. That sector was under the command of Brigadier General Robert Potter, who commanded a division in Major General Ambrose Burnside's Ninth Corps. Opposite Potter's position was situated a brigade of five South Carolina regiments under the command of Brigadier General Stephen Elliott. His brigade, along with a four-gun battery under the command of Captain Richard Pegram, occupied a salient that jutted out from the rest of Major General Bushrod Johnson's division under the command of Beauregard. Lieutenant Colonel Henry Pleasants of the Forty-eighth Pennsylvania, who had worked as a civil engineer before the war and now commanded the most advanced regiment in Potter's division, speculated that a mine could be dug under the enemy's salient and packed with explosives. Potter and Pleasants shared the idea with Burnside, who, once he believed the plan had a chance to succeed, passed the proposal up the chain of command to Meade and Grant. Meade authorized the construction of the mine even though he advocated a more traditional siege operation as opposed to costly frontal and flank assaults. Mining operations commenced on June 25 in a ravine removed from direct observation by the enemy and under the direct supervision of Sergeant Henry Reese.[7]

The men of the Forty-eighth Pennsylvania worked for one month, from the end of June to the third week in July, before completing a tunnel measuring roughly 500 feet, which branched off into two lateral chambers at a point under the Confederate fort. Once finished, the two chambers were packed with 320 kegs of gunpowder, totaling 8,000 pounds, and these were ready for detonation on July 28. Confederate countermines were attempted in the vicinity, but they proved to be too shallow. Pleasants believed he had "accomplished one of the great things of this war." He privately scoffed at the chief engineer and other "wiseacres" who failed to provide support for the operation or argued that a mine of such length was not feasible. Perhaps no one had a clearer sense than Pleasants of the mine's destructive power, and this manifested in his sense of foreboding: "It is terrible however, to hurl several men with my own hand at one blow into eternity, but I believe I am doing right."[8]

With the mine close to completion, the Union high command formulated a plan to exploit the results of what promised to be an impressive and destructive explosion. Burnside proposed using Brigadier General Edward Ferrero's division, which included two brigades of USCTs, to spearhead the attack and exploit what many believed would be a significant gap in the Confederate position. Ferrero's division was to push into the remains of the fort and swing left and right, sweeping the Confederate lines, followed by the other three divisions in Burnside's Ninth Corps. One division of the Tenth and one of the Eighteenth Corps stood ready to support the advance. Their goal was to break through the salient and seize a ridge crest overlooking Petersburg some 533 yards beyond. If all went as planned, black soldiers stood a chance of being the first Union soldiers to enter the city of Petersburg.[9]

The presence of African American soldiers signaled a dramatic shift in the overall policy of the Lincoln administration, which had hoped to save the Union strictly through military means without risking popular support by redrawing deeply entrenched racial boundaries. By the middle of the summer of 1862 it had become clear to military officials in the field and President Abraham Lincoln that both free and enslaved blacks could be utilized for military purposes to preserve the Union; to this end the president issued the Preliminary Emancipation Proclamation in September 1862 as well as authorization for the enlistment of blacks in the army. While the decision was intended both to increase troop strength and to cripple the Confederate war effort, Lincoln's decision fueled Northern prejudices and political opposition in 1863 both in the ranks and on the home front.[10]

Ferrero's "colored troops" were assigned to Burnside's Ninth Corps as part of its reorganization in January 1864. The division played a supporting role during the Overland campaign, though it skirmished briefly with Confederate forces on May 15 and 19. Throughout the campaign and into the trenches at Petersburg, black soldiers faced prejudice and discrimination, sometimes from their own white officers who, they believed, feared them as much as their former slave owners. Hard labor continued for Ferrero's men in the form of picket and fatigue duty as well as the construction of forts and breastworks. The prospect of actual combat and a chance to prove their battlefield prowess would have been eagerly anticipated by many of these men.[11]

The original plan to utilize Ferrero's Fourth Division as the vanguard of the Union assault remained in place until the afternoon prior to the attack, when Meade vetoed the use of black troops. While Meade worried that the public might accuse the army of needlessly sacrificing black men if the assault failed, the evidence suggests that he simply did not believe that inexperienced troops had a better chance of succeeding than veteran units. Burnside was devastated. He had carefully selected this unit not because the men were black but because they were fresh and had not been worn down by the monotony of life in the trenches. Meade amended Burnside's plan, instructing him to use his more experienced white divisions—with Ferrero's in support—to push straight through the breach in the Confederate lines and head for the crucial position of Cemetery Hill and the Jerusalem Plank Road, which overlooked Petersburg.[12]

Burnside was a competent commander when given specific instructions, but he found it difficult to improvise; now he was forced to make major revisions to his plan in the final hours preceding the assault. He

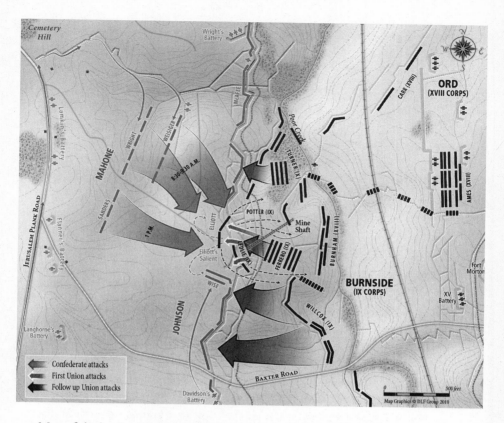

Map of the battle of the Crater, July 30, 1864. (David Fuller/DLF Group)

called on his other three division commanders. In addition to Potter's division, Brigadier Generals Orlando Willcox's and James Ledlie's divisions had been damaged to various degrees in the initial assaults on Petersburg. Burnside asked his three division commanders to draw lots from a hat to decide who would lead. Ledlie came up short and was given the assignment to lead the assault, even though he had already shown signs of incompetence, cowardice, and drunkenness. The final plan called for Ledlie's division to move into and through the crater with Willcox to follow on the left and Potter on the right to prevent the Confederates from counterattacking. Those units included Robert Ransom's North Carolina brigade, now under the command of Colonel Lee McAfee, on Elliott's left and Henry Wise's brigade, now under the command of Colonel John T. Goode, to his right. Artillery support was provided by Captain Richard Pegram's four-

The mine explosion from behind Union lines. (Robert Underwood Johnson and Clarence Clough Buel, *Battles and Leaders* [New York: Century, 1887–88], 4:561)

gun battery, positioned with Elliott's brigade. The assault was set for the early hours of July 30, with the mine to explode at 3:30 a.m.[13]

Because of a deficient fuse line, the explosion and subsequent attack set for 3:30 was delayed until roughly 4:44 a.m. Sergeant William Russell of Wise's brigade first "herd a tremendous dull report" and then "felt the earth shake beneath me." He described the immediate aftermath of the explosion as "an awful scene." Private John W. Haley in the Seventeenth Maine Regiment later described the explosion: "The most infernal din and uproar that ever greeted mortals crashed around us." The massive explosion left a hole in the ground 150 to 200 feet long, 60 feet wide, and 30 feet deep, and killed or wounded 278 men in Elliott's brigade plus 30 gunners in Pegram's battery.[14]

The paucity of accounts from Elliott's South Carolina brigade attests to the destructiveness of the explosion. Many were killed outright or buried alive in their sleep. Lieutenant Pursley of the Eighteenth South Carolina had just gone to sleep in a bombproof when "the first jar I felt I thought it was a boom had lit on my little boom proof. Just as I lit in to the ditch there came another blast & God only knows how high it sent me." With a bit of literary flair, Pursley described how "I spread out my wings to see if I could fly but the first thing I knowed I was lying on top of the works." In a letter to the parents of John W. Callahan of the Twenty-second South Carolina, Daniel Boyd conveyed the destructive power of the explosion by illustrating the conditions in which their son was discovered: "J W Calahan Was Kild by the blowing up of our breast Works he was buried wit[h] the dirt. When they found him he was Standing Straight up the ditch there was one hundred kild and buried with the explosion."[15]

The Union assault began with a massive artillery barrage along a front of nearly two miles. After a delay of somewhere between ten and fifteen minutes, Ledlie's two brigades, commanded by Brigadier General William F. Bartlett and Colonel Elisha G. Marshall, pushed toward the scene of the explosion, where they encountered a horrific sight. Rather than moving quickly through the crater and on to the vulnerable crest of Cemetery Hill, both brigades halted on the edge of the crater, in awe of the destruction and as a result of not having received orders from Ledlie to move quickly through the breach in the Confederate line. Precious time was wasted digging Confederates out of the dirt and collecting souvenirs from the dead. "The scene was horrible," recalled Stephen Weld. "Men were found half buried; some dead, some alive, some with their legs kicking in the air, some with the arms only exposed, and some with every bone in their bodies apparently broken." Eventually, the two brigades pushed farther and took up position on the far side of the crater. Brigade commanders seemed uncertain as to their goals, largely because of the absence of General Ledlie, who failed to accompany his men and instead removed himself to a bombproof, where he drank away the morning.[16]

Within thirty minutes of the explosion, Ledlie's men had maneuvered over the steep western wall of the crater and taken up a position in the complex chain of traverses that emanated out. One final push may have been sufficient to break the Confederate position, but Marshall's and Bartlett's brigades hesitated. At the same time Confederate batteries located in close proximity to the crater commenced with a deadly crossfire that frustrated plans for a further advance and prevented units from continuing to move into the vicinity. Adding to the Federals' difficulties, once the initial shock of the explosion had subsided, the remnants of Elliott's brigade and other Confederate units took up a defensive position in the shallow trenches and traverses and applied as much firepower on the advancing brigades as possible.

As Ledlie's division struggled to advance beyond the pit, the two brigades from Potter's Second Division, under the commands of Brigadier General Simon Griffin and Colonel Zenas Bliss, moved to a position just north of the crater to protect the First Division's right flank. Although the units were able to extend the overall front, they met fierce resistance from both the remainder of the Seventeenth South Carolina and Colonel McAfee's North Carolinians, who maneuvered into position to secure gaps in the line resulting from the extreme casualties in Elliott's brigade. Within a short time an officer in the Twenty-fifth North Carolina observed that the Federals "had planted seven stands of colors on our works." Meanwhile, on Ledlie's left the division of Orlando Willcox attacked, with the First Brigade under the command of Brigadier General John Hartranft in the lead. Hartranft's brigade occupied about 100 feet of trenches before Henry Wise's Virginia brigade, along with remnants of South Carolina units, checked it. Most of the men were pinned down in the pit with little room to maneuver or organize; as one Union soldier noted simply, it "proved more destructive to us than to the enemy." Within one hour of the mine explosion, close to 7,500 Union soldiers were defending a perimeter not much larger than the outlines of the crater itself. At the height of the Union assault, the three divisions advanced to occupy at least two separate Confederate lines beyond the confines of the crater.[17]

At approximately 8:00 a.m., the two brigades in Ferrero's Fourth Division were ordered into the mix. The First Brigade, under the command of Lieutenant Colonel Joshua K. Sigfried, led the way, with the Thirtieth USCT, under the command of Colonel Delavan Bates, in the vanguard. Once out of the Union lines, the brigade made its way over roughly 150 yards of open ground, all the while taking enfilading fire from Confederate rifles and artillery. A few of the lead units in the brigade were diverted to the right of the crater and into a maze of Confederate rifle pits and entrenchments, while the rest of the brigade was forced into the horror of the pit itself, which was quickly becoming a cauldron of death. Colonel Henry G. Thomas also faced the challenge of moving the Second Brigade away from the escalating bloodbath inside the crater, but was able to organize some of his men for an advance. Together, Thomas and Sigfried moved elements of their commands, along with scattered units in the vi-

The second Union wave included the division of USCTs under the command of Brigadier General Edward Ferrero. (Robert Underwood Johnson and Clarence Clough Buel, *Battles and Leaders* [New York: Century, 1887–88], 4:552)

cinity, into the confusing chain of rifle pits, trenches, and covered ways. As they made their way forward, they mistakenly fired on Griffin's men, who were still occupying the position they had taken as a result of their unsuccessful advance on Cemetery Hill earlier in the morning. Once in position, both Sigfried's and Thomas's brigades made an attempt to advance, but were met with stiff resistance.[18]

Any opportunity for a concerted advance was quickly lost as Brigadier General William Mahone arrived with two brigades from his division. Mahone's division was situated about one mile southwest of the crater at the time of the explosion, when he was ordered by Lee to move reinforcements to buttress the line. Mahone ordered Colonel David Weisiger's Virginia brigade and Lieutenant Colonel Matthew R. Hall's Georgia brigade to move to Cemetery Hill. These units advanced down the Jerusalem Plank Road until they turned east along a covered way to a ravine that branched north and west of the crater. As the two brigades rushed to take up position, Mahone ordered Brigadier General John C. C. Sanders's Alabama brigade to the front. Weisiger's Virginians took up a north-south line of battle that faced the crater to the east, with Hall's Georgians extending the line farther. At approximately 9:00 a.m., just as the advanced Union units were organizing a final assault toward the Jerusalem Plank Road, Weisiger was ordered forward by Mahone.[19]

Mahone's Virginians—along with scattered units of North and South Carolinians—were ordered to fix bayonets and not to fire until they reached the enemy line just 200 yards away. They immediately encountered the enemy and responded with heightened ferocity owing to the rumors that Ferrero's men were heard shouting, "Remember Fort Pillow!" and "No quarter!"—a reference to the reported execution of black soldiers in April 1864 at Fort Pillow, Tennessee. Weisiger's brigade engaged Ferrero's men as well as a handful of men in Griffin's brigade in close hand-to-hand fighting before the raw black soldiers were forced to retire back into the crater. "Instantly the whole body broke," recalled Bowley of the Thirtieth USCT, "and went over the breastworks toward the Union line, or ran down the trenches towards the crater." As Weisiger pushed his men in pursuit of the now-retreating Federals, Mahone ordered Hall's Georgia brigade to attack against the southern rim of the crater. Its initial attack repulsed, the brigade was forced to take up a position behind Weisiger.[20]

At 1:00 p.m. Mahone ordered Sanders's Alabama brigade into the mix. The 630 men in this unit were able to advance directly to the rim of the crater, forcing Union commanders to scrap any attempt at an orderly retreat. Desperate hand-to-hand fighting ensued within the heated cauldron as both white and black Union soldiers attempted to maintain some semblance of order. The attack proved to be the final assault of the battle; Confederates gradually gained control of the crater as Union soldiers either surrendered or in desperation attempted to flee back to their lines. An open field of some 100 yards, according to a soldier in the Fifty-first New York Infantry, "was completely swept by the enemy's Artillery and Infantry, some few of them tried it but the most of those that made the attempt were either killed or wounded." Federal units stationed in between the crater and their own lines were given the job of slowing down the stream of frightened white and black soldiers. Black troops who surrendered as well as white officers who commanded black units faced an uncertain future.[21]

The official report identified 3,826 Union casualties out of 16,722 engaged, comprising 504 killed or mortally wounded, 1,881 wounded, and 1,441 missing and presumed to be prisoners of war. Ferrero's Fourth

Division accounted for 41 percent of the total casualties, though it constituted only 21 percent of the men engaged. Confederate casualties were significantly lighter. Out of a total force of roughly 10,000 engaged at the Crater, 361 were killed or mortally wounded, 727 wounded, and 403 missing.[22]

In the days following the battle, the two armies reorganized and worked feverishly to extend their earthworks, while the men who took part in the fight attempted to make sense of an experience that deviated sharply from previous battles. Surviving letters and diaries follow a pattern in their tendency to concentrate on specific themes that emerged as a result of the scale of the initial explosion and the violent combat that took place on a landscape turned otherworldly by the large chunks of soil, body parts, and debris scattered about.

Soldiers recalled in great detail the nature of the fighting in and around the crater. The close proximity of the fighting was due in large part to the size of the pit created by the explosion, along with adjacent earthworks and traverses, and the nature of the Union attack itself, which left a large percentage of its men confined within the crater's outer rim and packed tightly within the extended earthworks. David Holt of the Sixteenth Mississippi judged the battle to be the "most horrible sight that even old veterans . . . had ever seen" and compared it to "the bloody ditch at Spotsylvania and the Yankee breastworks at Chancellorsville." For the men in Union ranks confined within the crater itself there was both the constant pressure of Confederate resistance as well as highly accurate artillery. Brigadier General William Bartlett, who was taken prisoner at the end of the battle, recalled that the enemy "threw bayonets and bottles on us" while John Haley felt as though "every gun in the defense of Petersburg swept that spot."[23]

Accounts of the battlefield after the fighting ended attest to the brutality of the combat within a closely defined area of the landscape around Elliott's Salient. Lee's men were forced to rebuild their lines while they buried large numbers of comrades as well as the enemy. "After the Battle was over they were lying in our entrenchments in piles blacks whites," recalled Lieutenant Colonel Matthew Love of the Twenty-fifth North Carolina, "and all together lying in piles three and four deep." Private Dorsey Binion of the Forty-eighth Georgia Infantry painted a graphic picture of the battlefield for his sister: "The whole face of the works was litterly strewn with dead negroes and our men."[24]

The delays in agreeing to the terms of a truce added to the ghastly sights that soldiers on both sides witnessed and recorded. The men were unable to reach out to their wounded comrades until the morning of August 1; the hot temperatures and grueling summer sun added to the number of deaths during those crucial hours. Soldiers detailed to collect the dead, such as Hamilton Dunlap of the 100th Pennsylvania Infantry, were forced to use their shovels to pick up the bodies, which by then "were all maggot-eaten." Only in death were racial distinctions no longer observable: "Men cut in a thousand pieces and as black as your hat! You could not tell the white from the black by their hair." Adam Henry recalled wandering the battlefield but quickly succumbed to the "awful Smell" emanating from a pile of 300 corpses, which had severely deteriorated owing to the scalding heat and sun.[25]

While the scale of violence witnessed at the Crater fit into the broader narrative of a war whose brutality had surpassed what many believed possible in 1861, the presence of USCTs constituted a fundamental shift in the conflict for the men in the Army of the Potomac and the Army of Northern Virginia. For black Union soldiers in the Ninth Corps, their inclusion in the operation offered them the most direct opportunity to assist in the destruction of slavery. In doing so, they would not only help preserve the Union but push the barriers that prevented them from enjoying the benefits and civil rights of full citizenship. Such a scenario was only possible if black men asserted themselves on the battlefield in a full demonstration of their worth as soldiers and as men. By 1864 the battlefield had become a dangerous proposition for black Union soldiers following the announcement from Confederate officials that black soldiers would be treated as slaves and their white officers executed for inciting slave rebellion. As the men of the Fourth Division moved into position late in the evening of July 29, they were encouraged to "Remember Fort Pillow."[26]

Black Union soldiers shared in the disappointment surrounding defeat with their comrades in the other three divisions, though their bravery on the battlefield was demonstrated in the high casualty count as well as their participation in some of the farthest advances to take place on the morning of July 30. Unfortunately, the historical record is slim owing to their heavy losses as well as the high illiteracy rates that characterized "colored" regiments. The handful of accounts that are available highlight the harsh treatment accorded to black troops at the hands of Confederates. Sergeant Rodney Long of the Twenty-ninth USCT, who spent seven months imprisoned in Danville, Virginia, recounted that he and his comrades "suffered terribly." Fellow inmate Isaac Gaskin recalled, "I was punished severely on account of my color" and estimated that out of 180 colored prisoners only 7 survived the ordeal.[27]

Although accounts from the survivors of Ferrero's division describe the horrors of battle and the experience of witnessing comrades executed following their surrender, they do not lose sight of the broader collective goal. Survivors of the Crater as well as other campaigns viewed their sacrifice and valor on the battlefield as an integral component in a transformation of American society that would ultimately result in the rights of full citizenship. A soldier in the Forty-third USCT stated proudly, "No longer can it be said that we have no rights in the country in which we live because we have never marched forward to its defense," while a comrade took pleasure in the fact that he had "helped sustain the nation's pride." Chaplain White of the Twenty-eighth USCT looked even further into the future, anticipating that "the historian's pen cannot fail to locate us somewhere among the good and great, who have fought and bled upon the altar of their country."[28]

African American men in the ranks understood that a broad transformation in beliefs among white Americans would not come about easily as they struggled for recognition on the battlefield. They received little notice from Northern newspapers, which reported on their presence in passing if they were mentioned at all. What coverage there was tended to fall along political lines. The *Leavenworth Conservative* praised their performance in the face of overwhelming resistance and fire while the Democratic *Putnam County Courier* of Carmel, New York, declared: "Nothing in the details of the battle yet received tends to extenuate the conduct of the negro troops, or to relieve the officers having immediate direction of the operation, from the accusations of blundering." Most were influenced by accounts from the field, which offered minimal praise of the performance of USCTs. The *Christian Recorder* reported, "The enemy finally succeeded in causing a panic in the sable ranks" while the *Baltimore Sun* proclaimed in bold print, "The Colored Troops Falter." Readers of Philadelphia's *Daily Evening Bulletin* would have been hard-pressed to find anything positive in the paper's coverage of the movements of the Fourth Division: "Their officers cheered them on; they moved a little further forward, again faltered, were again urged to go forward by their officer; still they faltered; entreaties changed

Private Louis E. Martin of Company E, Twenty-ninth
USCT, a former slave from Arkansas who enlisted in Illinois, lost his right arm and left leg at the Crater. (RG94,
Records of the Adjutant General's Office, National Archives, Washington, D.C.)

to threats, but both were alike useless." Rare was the favorable coverage
found in *Harper's Weekly* on August 20. The reporter praised USCTs for
their performance at Petersburg, inquiring of readers "whether any soldiers
would have fought more steadfastly and bravely and willingly than the
colored troops in the Union army?"[29]

Negative portrayals of USCTs' fighting abilities or no newspaper coverage at all reflected deeply ingrained racial prejudices that were pervasive throughout the North. The appointment of white officers to command black soldiers was intended to assuage these racial concerns about the physical, mental, and moral character of black soldiers, but although these men were positioned to work as advocates for USCTs, they often succumbed to the very same prejudices. Very few officers originated from within abolitionist circles; most no doubt hoped to take advantage of the opportunity for increased pay as well as promotion in rank. Mixed motivations and the desire to reassure their families as well as the general public of their own competency as officers led to mixed reviews. "They went up as well as I ever saw troops," claimed Colonel Henry G. Thomas, but then he qualified his praise: "They came back very badly. They came back on the run, every man for himself." Captain James A. Rickard, who served in the Nineteenth USCT, asserted, "The charge of Ferrero's division . . . and temporary capture of their interior works . . . is a record to win back the previously prejudiced judgment of the president, cabinet generals, and officers of the Army of the Potomac, who up to this time had thought negroes all right for service in menial capacity." With the exception of some officers who were able to cast off much of their racism to develop strong relationships with black men and acknowledge their worth as soldiers, it is likely that the assessments of most white commanders were based on facile observations that merely solidified long-standing assumptions.[30]

While the assessment of white officers was mixed regarding the USCTs' performance at the Crater, there was very little ambivalence outside of the Fourth Division in soldiers' general opinions of how the battle had been conducted. Soldiers shared their frustrations in letters to family members back home, threatening not to reenlist or vowing to vote for the Democratic nominee in the upcoming presidential election. More specifically, soldiers in the other three Ninth Corps divisions and throughout the Army of the Potomac directed their frustrations at the Union high command, including generals Meade, Grant, and Burnside. A soldier in the Thirty-fifth Massachusetts was convinced that "there were men enough to eat the Rebs up if they had been put in" but concluded that jealousy prevented Meade from fully supporting Burnside's attack. A soldier in the Seventeenth Maine observed that "with Grant in command we have been in front of Petersburg as long, aye longer than McClellan sat in front of

Richmond." Compared to Grant, this soldier opined, McClellan was a "humane general and tried to avoid useless slaughter of his men."[31]

Added to the deep-seated racial prejudices already present within the ranks, the emotional pains of defeat and the growing sense of frustration with the course of the war made it easy to place the blame for the disaster at the Crater at the feet of the USCTs. A soldier in the Thirty-sixth Massachusetts spoke for many of his white comrades when he observed that the USCTs "skedaddled" in the face of Confederate pressure and went on to suggest, "If it hadn't been for them we should have occupied Petersburg yesterday." Although Charles Mills praised the leadership of the white officers, he noted that the black troops "were not worth a straw to resist" and "ran like sheep." "A short delay of an hour, of a single hour, or the unaccountable panic that seized the niggers," recalled Edward Cook in the 100th New York Infantry, "lost us a battle, which if it had been gained by us, would have proved to be the most important and decisive one of the campaign either in this department or any other." He concluded, "Everybody here is down on the niggers." Such language worked to confirm white soldiers' own assumptions about the physical and moral shortcomings of black men, assumptions that many on the home front, grown weary of war, reinforced.[32]

Union soldiers focused specifically on the "panic-stricken retreat" of the USCTs as the moment when the battle was lost, but failed to include the fact that various units had managed to maneuver themselves in a forward position just as Mahone's counterattack began. Many white soldiers, such as Edward Whitman of the Third Division, captured the moment by characterizing the soldiers as "terror-stricken darkies" who "dropped their arms and fled without dealing a blow, embarrassing the white troops around them." One soldier wrote openly of an order to "fix Baonetts to stop" the retreating soldiers, and Edward Cook suggested that the heavy casualty count was caused in part by "white troops firing into the retreating niggers." Cook may have been referring to an incident, which took place after Mahone's charge, that left both white and black soldiers hopelessly trapped in the crater. According to George Kilmer, his fellow white soldiers were seized with panic "that the enemy would give no quarter to negroes, or to the whites taken with them." "It has been positively asserted," continued Kilmer, "that white men bayoneted blacks who fell back into the crater . . . in order to preserve the whites from Confederate vengeance." The inordinate amount of blame leveled at one of the four divisions participating in the assault suggests that serious racial prejudice still existed among the troops, notwithstanding the growing acceptance that the abolition of slavery was necessary to maintain the Union.[33]

Albeit for very different reasons, Confederate soldiers who fought at the Crater also achieved a remarkable level of consensus as they assessed the fighting that took place on July 30. The novelty of the mine explosion under unsuspecting soldiers in the predawn hours confirmed to most Confederates, as well as those who read about the battle in newspapers, that the Lincoln administration and the North had abandoned any sense of morality and decency. The relative ease with which Confederates were able to retake the salient translated into a firm belief that Grant's formidable host could be resisted at least for the immediate future. In addition, their overwhelming faith that General Lee could successfully resist Grant's offensives around Petersburg left open the possibility that Northern voters might grow weary of a protracted war and replace Lincoln with someone else (perhaps George B. McClellan) in the November election. Such a result might ultimately lead to peace and independence. John F. Sale, who served in the Twelfth Virginia, asserted that although "he [Grant] has a tremendous army" and "has outnumbered us two to one all this time . . . , for all that he has gained no decided advantage."[34]

More important, the presence of an entire division of armed black men in blue uniform on a battlefield situated near a large civilian population proved decisive in shaping the accounts penned by the men in the Army of Northern Virginia in the wake of the battle. The massacre of USCTs by Confederates at the Crater, as well as how they assessed the presence of black soldiers, must be understood within a broader narrative of slave insurrection and the perceived threat to a social, political, and economic hierarchy based on white supremacy. The consensus achieved in their post-battle accounts can best be understood when analyzed as an extension of long-standing fears attached to the constant threat that armed blacks posed throughout the antebellum period and the roles and responsibilities that white Southerners—slaveholding and nonslaveholding alike—assumed in maintaining a slave-based society.

The responsibilities that white Southerners assumed in defending their families from armed black men had roots in their collective memories and, most important, their fears, both real and imagined, of slave insurrections that had been shaped over the course of the nineteenth century by events in the United States and abroad. While Nat Turner's deadly insurrection in Southampton County, Virginia, in August 1831, which took the lives of over sixty men, women, and children, loomed large, white Southerners (especially slaveholders) also remembered failed attempts in Richmond led by Gabriel Prosser (1801) and in South Carolina by Denmark Vesey (1823) and closely followed the news from the West Indies. This was an area that experienced continual violence in places like Barbados (1816) and Demerera (1823). The steps taken by British abolitionists to end slavery in this region helped to reinforce assumptions held by white Southerners regarding how to understand and prevent slave unrest. Most important, the agreement among slaveholders in the Caribbean that agitators in England were to blame for slave unrest provided slave owners in the United States with a rationale for the actions of their own supposedly loyal and obedient slaves.[35]

Turner's insurrection reinforced a need for vigilance that did not compromise paternalistic assumptions that white Southerners believed bound them to their slaves. It was no coincidence that Turner's actions occurred shortly after the publication of William Lloyd Garrison's *Liberator* in January 1831, and slaveholders were quick to point the finger. Even after Turner's capture and execution, fears did not subside as news spread of another insurrection in Jamaica involving 60,000 slaves followed closely by the decision of the British Parliament to abolish the institution throughout the empire.[36]

The sectional disputes of the 1840s and 1850s offered a continual reminder of the dangers posed by outside agitators and a hostile federal government. Slave patrols and state laws were meant to delineate racial boundaries and exercise tighter control of the region's black population and consequently bound white Southerners ever more closely to one another. John Brown's raid at Harpers Ferry in October 1859 and the election of the nation's first "black" Republican as president convinced many in the slaveholding South of the necessity of secession as the only solution that could protect the institution of slavery and ensure their own continued security. The men who defended Petersburg and its civilian population on that hot July day not only understood the nature of the threat that black soldiers posed but, more important, they understood what needed to be done in response.[37]

Lee's officers and men were already engaged in heated combat by the time Ferrero's division entered the battle. For the survivors of Elliott's South Carolina brigade, as well as the other units in the immediate vicinity of the Crater, the first sign of the black troops was their battle cry. Thomas Smith vividly recalled that the men "charged me crying no quarter, remember Fort Pillow." The majority of Confederate accounts include references to Fort Pillow, though it is impossible to know how many actually heard such a battle cry given the noise and confusion on the battlefield. The sight of the black soldiers alone would have been sufficient to change the very nature of the reaction of Lee's men. "It had the same affect upon our men that a red flag had upon a mad bull," was the way one South Carolinian who survived the initial explosion described the reaction of his comrades. David Holt of the Sixteenth Mississippi remembered, "They were the first we had seen and the sight of a nigger in a blue uniform and with a gun was more than 'Johnnie Reb' could stand. Fury had taken possession" of Holt, and "I knew that I felt as ugly as they looked." Anyone with even a modicum of experience reading Civil War letters and diaries appreciates that soldiers rarely shied away from conveying to loved ones the horrors of battle and their hatred of the enemy, but in this case it is important to keep in mind that Confederates did not perceive USCTs as soldiers. The harsh language used to describe black soldiers not only worked to dehumanize these individuals, it also opened up the possibility of violent and swift retaliation.[38]

Many Confederates relished the opportunity to share their experiences in the Crater fighting Ferrero's division and they did so in a way that bordered on cathartic. The vivid descriptions suggest that this killing was of a different kind, given the nature of the enemy. These men were perceived as slaves and by extension fell outside the boundary of ordinary rules of warfare. "Our men killed them with the bayonets and the but[t]s of there guns and every other way," according to Laban Odom, who served in the Forty-eighth Georgia, "until they were lying eight or ten deep on top of one enuther and the blood almost s[h]oe quarter deep." Another soldier in the Forty-eighth Georgia described the hand-to-hand combat: "The Bayonet was plunged through their hearts & the muzzle of our guns was put on their temple & their brains blown out others were knocked in the head with butts of our guns. Few would succeed in getting to the rear safe."[39]

Both the horror of battle and rage at having to fight black soldiers must have been apparent to the mother of one soldier when she learned that her son "shot them down until we got mean enough and then rammed them through with the Bayonet." Another soldier admitted, "Some few negroes went to the rear as we could not kill them as fast as they past us."

Lieutenant Colonel William Pegram described in great detail for his wife situations in which black soldiers "threw down ther arms to surrender, but were not allowed to do so. Every bombproof I saw had one or two dead negroes in them, who had skulked out of the fight, & been found & killed by our men." The sharing of these incidents with loved ones back home reinforced the connection between the battlefield and home front and provided soldiers with a clear understanding of what they were defending their families from. White Southerners may have been especially vivid in their recollections to the females in their families as a reminder of what emancipation would likely mean to their physical safety and honor.[40]

The use of black Union soldiers served as a rallying cry for Confederates who did not participate in the battle; writing about the battle served as an outlet through which they could express their resentment and anger over the use of black soldiers. Describing how "our men bayoneted them & knacked ther bra[i]ns with the but[t] of their guns," as did Lee Barfield, may have been the next most satisfying thing to being there. Even A. T. Fleming, who served in the Tenth Alabama but missed the battle due to illness, could not help but allow his racist preconceptions to pervade a very descriptive account in which Confederates "knocked them in the head like killing hogs." Perhaps commenting on the dead black soldiers on the battlefield or the prisoners, Fleming described them as the "Blackest greaysest [greasiest] negroes I ever saw in my life." Stationed at Bermuda Hundred during the battle, Edmund Womack wrote home to his wife, "I understand our men just chopped them to pieces." For the soldiers who did not take part in the fight at the Crater, sharing battle stories with families bound them more closely with those who did and brought to life the emancipation policies of the Lincoln administration.[41]

Once the salient was retaken, Confederate rage was difficult to bring under control. Accounts written in the days following the battle rarely shied away from including vivid descriptions of the harsh treatment and executions of surrendered black soldiers. Jerome B. Yates of the Sixteenth Mississippi recalled, "Most of the Negroes were killed after the battle. Some was killed after they were taken to the rear." "The only sounds which now broke the silence," according to Henry Van Lewvenigh Bird, "was some poor wounded wretch begging for water and quieted by a bayonet thrust which said unmistakably 'Bois ton sang. Tu n'aurais de soif' [Drink your blood. You will have no more thirst]." James Verdery simply described "a truly *Bloody Sight a perfect Massacre nearly* a Black flag fight." It would be a mistake to reduce these accounts to examples of uncontrolled rage in the face of these black combatants. The level of violence exhibited toward black Union soldiers served no tactical purpose, but allowed Confederates to vent their fury in the face of what they perceived to be a racial order turned upside down and a direct threat to their own communities and families. Indeed, the proximity of the battlefield to the city of Petersburg would have given Confederates a clear sense that they were defending a civilian population from a slave uprising, which further fueled their anger.[42]

We should not interpret the massacre of black soldiers at the Crater as simply a function of collective rage; rather, it should be viewed as a measured response. Analyzing the Confederate response at the Crater alongside slave rebellions extending back to the beginning of the nineteenth century opens up the possibility of a more nuanced explanation. An 1816 rebellion on the island of Barbados resulted in the execution of roughly 200 slaves, and in Demerera (1823) another 200 slaves were executed following a failed rebellion. Closer to Petersburg, roughly 200 slaves were either publicly tortured or executed following Turner's Rebellion in 1831. Such violent responses served a number of purposes. Most notably they sent a strong message to the slave community of who was in control, that such behavior would not be tolerated, and that such actions had no hope of succeeding. A direct and brutal response would also work to drain any remaining enthusiasm for rebellion. Applying this framework to the Crater allows us to move beyond the mere fact of rage to better discern the intended consequences of the scale of the violence meted out to black soldiers.[43]

The lessons of Turner and Brown also convinced white Southerners that unless agitated by meddling abolitionists, their slaves were content and would remain loyal. Such a view provided an avenue for Confederates to explain away apparent acts of bravery and skill exhibited on the battlefield on the part of USCTs. John C. C. Sanders, who commanded the Alabama brigade in Mahone's division, was forced to admit that the "Negroes . . . fight much better than I expected." However, he was quick to qualify this statement with the conviction that "they were driven on by the Yankees and many of them were shot down by the latter." Any acknowledgment of soldierly qualities in USCTs threatened long-standing assumptions regarding the dependent nature of the black race and the paternal justification for slavery itself. J. Edward Peterson, who served as a band member in the Twenty-sixth North Carolina, described the black soldiers at the Crater as "ignorant" and like Sanders assumed they were forced to fight by the Yankees. Perhaps in light of a paternalistic self-perception, Peterson went on to conclude that because of this they did not deserve such harsh treatment by Confederates following the battle. Peterson seems to be one of few who held this view.[44]

Not surprisingly, as a result of their experience fighting black soldiers, many Confederates experienced a renewed sense of purpose and commitment to the cause. Years after the war, Edward Porter Alexander remembered that the "general feeling of the men towards their employment was very bitter." According to Alexander, "The sympathy of the North for John Brown's memory was taken for proof of a desire that our slaves should rise in a servile insurrection & massacre throughout the South, & the enlistment of Negro troops was regarded as advertisement of that desire & encouragement of the idea to the Negro." Paul Higginbotham of the Nineteenth Virginia reminded his relatives back home that many of his comrades believed that "old Abe will be defeated for President. . . . I am confident we will yet again gain our independence," asserted this soldier defiantly, "if we are true to our cause and Country." William Pegram also acknowledged the perceived threat when he noted, "I had been hoping that the enemy would bring some negroes against this army." And now that they had, "I am convinced . . . that it has a splendid effect on our men." Pegram concluded that though "it seems cruel to murder them in cold blood," the men who did it had "very good cause for doing so." According to Pegram's most recent biographer, the experience facing black troops during the war renewed his commitment to the values of the antebellum world, "which had given birth and meaning to his nationalistic beliefs." The reflections of all three men suggest that Confederates identified closely with one another, their communities, and the Confederate nation. The experience of fighting black soldiers for the first time served to remind Lee's men of exactly what was at stake in the war—nothing less than an overturning of the racial hierarchy of their antebellum world.[45]

Newspapers published in the days after the battle echoed the enthusiasm of the men in Lee's army; editors used the occasion to remind their readers of the sacrifices being made in the trenches of Petersburg and went to great lengths to encourage their readers to remain optimistic and supportive of military efforts in hopes that further victories might lead to a Lincoln defeat in November. Inevitably, newspaper accounts of the battle referenced the presence of USCTs in a way that reinforced the themes already present in the letters and diaries of the soldiers. Most accounts used the widely reported screams of "No quarter!" to justify the response of Confederate soldiers both on the battlefield and in the immediate aftermath. An editorial in a Petersburg newspaper noted the war cry, concluding, "Our brave boys took them at their word and gave them what they had so loudly called for—'*no quarter.*'"[46]

The *Richmond Times* included a great deal of commentary that referenced the presence of black soldiers in the battle both to warn its readers of possible dangers and as a means to maintain support for the war effort. Readers on the home front were made aware of the dangers that black soldiers represented and, by extension, the dangers posed by their own slaves. "Negroes, stimulated by whiskey, may possibly fight well so long so they fight successfully," continued the report, "but with the first good whipping, their courage, like that of Bob Acres, oozes out at their fingers' ends." The attempt to deny black manhood by assuming they had to be "stimulated by whiskey" to fight reinforced stereotypes, while the reference to "whipping" took on a dual meaning between the battlefield and home front as a way to maintain racial control. In addition, the North's use of black troops allowed the newspaper to draw a sharp distinction between "heartless Yankees" who would stoop to a "barbarous device for adding horrors to the war waged against the South" and "Robert E. Lee, the soldier without reproach, and the Christian gentleman without stain and without dishonor." Emphasizing Lee's unblemished moral character highlighted his role as the Confederacy's best hope for independence even as he served as a model for the rest of the white South to emulate as the enemy took the ominous step of introducing black troops.[47]

The *Richmond Examiner* not only acknowledged the execution of black Union soldiers but went a step further and encouraged Mahone to continue the practice in the future: "We beg him [Mahone], hereafter, when negroes are sent forward to murder the wounded, and come shouting 'no quarter,' shut your eyes, General, strengthen your stomach with a little brandy and water, and let the work, which God has entrusted to you and your brave men, go forward to its full completion; that is, until every negro has been slaughtered.—Make every salient you are called upon to defend, a Fort Pillow; butcher every negro that Grant sends against your brave troops, and permit them not to soil their hands with the capture of a single hero."[48]

Newspapers portrayed Lee's men as the only obstacle preventing the slaughter of innocent civilians at the hands of uncontrollable former slaves who had been duped into fighting their previous masters. The *Richmond Examiner* editorial acknowledged the emotional difficulty attached to such behavior, since under normal circumstances blacks should be treated according to the paternal instincts that white Southerners claimed to exercise in the management of their slaves. In the wake of the Crater, however, it was necessary for Lee and his men to stand firm in preventing Nat Turner writ large.

The use of USCTs at the Crater and elsewhere signaled a dramatic shift in the war aims of the United States: from the preservation of the Union in 1861 to a policy that began the process of emancipation and the integration of black Americans more fully into the civic circle. For the men who fought the battle, their initial reactions not only reflected their respective positions on this policy but also anticipated future promises as well as fears. White Southerners, both in the ranks and on the home front, confronted the manifestation of their worst fears in armed black men who, in aiding the Union cause, worked toward the destruction of the Confederacy as well as a way of life built around slavery. On the other hand, while white Union soldiers may have accepted the necessity of abolishing slavery on moral grounds and as a military necessity, their assessment of the performance of their fellow black soldiers suggests that entrenched racial perceptions would continue to influence their judgments. As a unit, the USCTs suffered the highest percentage of casualties of any division that participated in the battle. They also received a disproportionate share of the blame for the defeat from their white comrades and faced unspeakable violence at the hands of their enemy. Nonetheless, black Union soldiers remained fixed on ultimate victory for the nation and embraced the hope that it would lead to the end of slavery and greater civic inclusiveness.

| Chapter 2 |

THE LOST CAUSE
Maintaining the Antebellum Hierarchy

WILLIAM E. CAMERON was born and raised in Petersburg, Virginia. He served in the Twelfth Virginia Infantry and, like the rest of the men in the regiment, who hailed from the city and surrounding region, fought desperately on the morning of July 30, 1864, to protect his family and community from the Federal army and the myriad horrors associated with the presence of United States Colored Troops. By April 1865 Cameron could be found promoting the Confederate government's new policy of recruiting slaves to serve as soldiers in experimental all-black regiments. Such a drastic shift in policy reflected not only the military situation in Virginia and elsewhere, which was now critical, but also the steps that white Southerners were willing to take to preserve the institution of slavery.[1]

With the surrender of the Army of Northern Virginia at Appomattox Court House on April 9, 1865, Cameron and his comrades began the difficult transition back to civilian life, attempting to heal both the physical and psychological scars of war as well as learn to live with the changes relating to the abolition of slavery and Reconstruction. For the white residents of Petersburg, defeat meant military occupation under the command of Major General George Lucas Hartsuff and, for a time, the presence of Brigadier General Edward Ferrero's division. While Petersburg remained relatively peaceful in the immediate postwar years, many former Confederates harbored deep resentment associated with defeat and the radical change to the racial hierarchy.[2]

Residents made little formal attempt to preserve the many miles of earthworks that ringed the city. A few establishments—most notably Jarratt's Hotel—as well as the owner of the site of the Crater attempted to attract tourists to the remaining battlefields as part of a broader appeal to middle-class genteel culture, but public officials and town boosters apparently did not view the preservation of its Civil War experience as central to the city's economic future or as something that might be consumed by the general public. This is not surprising given the expansiveness of the earthworks themselves, the need to return land to its prewar agricultural use, and the many challenges associated with an expanding urban landscape. Although the steps taken to transform the Crater into a landscape appropriate for genteel touring paled in comparison with Gettysburg, by the 1870s modern pilgrims enjoyed easy access to select sites, as a growing obsession with battlefield relics quickly assumed a sacred quality.[3]

Only gradually did the veterans of the war, including William Mahone's Virginia brigade, take an active interest in commemorating and remembering the battle through reunions and written accounts. As early as the end of the 1870s a consensus concerning the battle of the Crater had been achieved, which included an emphasis on the heroics of the Virginia brigade and William Mahone specifically. More important, the memory of USCTs at the Crater had been minimized or, more often than not, shaped to conform to changing racial boundaries in postwar Virginia.

For the farmers in the Petersburg area whose land had been destroyed by the intricate network of trenches, the task of returning to conditions suitable for cultivation commenced in earnest. For many, the earthworks constituted an obstacle to this process of rebuilding. One exception to this could be found on the farm of William H. Griffith, who owned the ground on which the famous battle was fought.

Visitors to battlefields in the first few years following the war were driven more by curiosity than by an interest in formal remembrance. For many, the site of a battlefield engendered a visceral connection to the scenes that could only be read about in newspapers or witnessed in dramatic illustrations and photographs. The reactions of tourists reflected the wide gap between parlor-room musings concerning battle and the brute facts that greeted visitors upon arrival.

One of the earliest visitors to the Petersburg battlefields arrived just as Lee's army surrendered at Appomattox. Thomas Kennard and his son had recently arrived in New York City from England on a business trip when they accepted an offer to travel by steam sloop to City Point, Virginia. From there they made their way to Petersburg, where the ten-month siege

This is the earliest known photograph of the Crater (ca. 1865). (RG985-CWP27.27, U.S. Army Military History Institute, Carlisle Barracks, Pennsylvania)

had been broken only days before. "The city presented the most desolate appearance—public buildings, warehouses, private houses, &c., too clearly bore evidence of the effects of the heavy shelling," wrote Kennard. It is unknown whether Kennard traversed the Crater site, though it can be assumed that his description of the battlefields would have applied to it: "The dead were buried on the plain, but in the trenches numbers were lying as they fell during the assault, nearly all being shot through the head." Kennard and his son were treated to a view of the battlefield that few civilians would have experienced.[4]

Within a few short years, many of the more elaborate positions along the Petersburg lines, such as Fort Mahone and Fort Morton, had been leveled. As early as 1867 a visitor to the Petersburg battlefields noted, "At present the lines are little more than imaginary lines, broke here and there by embankments and trenches filled up by the plow of the husbandman." Another visitor predicted, "In a few years the great bulk of these works will have been plowed and dug down." The early removal of the earth-works dotting the landscape around the city of Petersburg left the Crater as one of the few intact wartime sites.[5]

In the years after the war, increased numbers of middle- and upper-class Northerners made their way south to enjoy the health benefits of natural springs as well as to experience what was left of the Old South. Tourism of the Crater and other Petersburg sites was encouraged by Jar-ratt's Hotel, considered one of the more luxurious destinations for travelers in the area. Jarratt's published a handbook authored by a former engineer officer in the Union army for use by visitors as they toured what remained of the battlefields. The handbook included an outline of the ten-month siege, a map indicating the important sites, and a travel narrative written by the editor of the *American Agriculturist,* who had toured the area in June 1865. Jarratt's not only hoped to encourage tourism but also planned to leave its guests with an "intelligent idea of the siege, the position of the two armies, [and] the character of the tremendous defensive works which cover the country about the city." In 1869 a revised pamphlet was pub-lished by the hotel under the direction of its new owner, Confederate veteran Phillip F. Brown. This revised version included the original fea-tures in addition to Lee's General Orders No. 9, an account of prisoners of war, and poetry. Local designers Thomas Morgan and Anthony Dibrell of Petersburg rounded out the pamphlet with a lithograph depicting the last national flag of the Confederacy encircled by notable scenes of the war.[6]

Northern journalist John T. Trowbridge—who included Petersburg on his Southern tour in September 1865—hoped to chronicle the South's adjustment to a free-labor society. While touring the Crater, Trowbridge was able to locate the mouth of the mine tunnel as well as the Confederate countermine. "In spots the surface earth had caved, leaving chasms open-ing into the mine along its course," recalled Trowbridge. The field was still littered with rusted bayonets and canteens, "and all around were graves." Upon noticing a "Negro man and woman" digging for bullets in the vicinity of the Crater, Trowbridge was told that "they got four cents a pound for them in Petersburg." Russell Conwell, who had served in the Union army, visited Petersburg in 1869 to tour what was left of the battle-fields. For a veteran, the sudden disappearance of the sights and smells of war could not pass without comment. "The logs that our boys tugged to the front, for an abutment in the earthworks, are now being used for kin-dling wood in the fashionable residences of Petersburg." As for the various

Griffith Farm. William H. Griffith operated a museum and charged admission to visit the remains of the Crater. His preservation efforts stood in sharp contrast to the economic development that quickly threatened the earthworks that ringed Petersburg. (U.S. Army Military History Institute, Carlisle Barracks, Pennsylvania)

types of shells that had once littered the ground, Conwell was told they "are fast being melted into ploughshares and machinery and the missiles of war become the instruments of peace." "All is changed there now," recalled the hero of Little Round Top, Joshua L. Chamberlain, on a visit in 1882. "What was a solid piece of works through which I led my troops is now all cleared field, & the hill side so smooth there is now grown up with little clumps of trees—marking some spots made more rich perhaps by the bloody struggles enacted on them."[7]

William H. Griffith, who owned the farm on which the battle took place, responded quickly to the financial opportunities of increased visitation. He fenced off the site of the explosion and laid out flagstone paths leading to the crater. By 1867 an admission fee of 25¢ helped pay for steps leading to the crater, a "Crater Saloon" where visitors could refresh themselves, and a small museum housing relics from the battle. On more than one occasion veterans of the battle refused to pay the entrance fee—it was known that Griffith rarely resisted, especially if the individual in question was a Confederate veteran. There can be little doubt that Griffith's im-

Earthworks north of the crater after the war. (Military Order of the Loyal Legion, U.S. Army Military History Institute, Carlisle Barracks, Pennsylvania)

provements preserved much of the crater site. One visitor in 1870 commented that "the earthen forts remain with little change."[8]

Griffith's improvements proved attractive enough to entice a wide range of visitors to the battlefield. More notable visitors who signed one of two register books included former Confederate general officers James Longstreet, Fitzhugh Lee, Henry Heth, and Edward Porter Alexander. Union generals included George Stoneman, Abner Doubleday, and Rufus Ingalls. Visitors from outside the ranks ranged from George Bancroft to Edward E. Hale to Thomas Nelson Page. Private ownership and accompanying financial reward due to public curiosity ensured that the Crater would not meet the same fate as other military sites around Petersburg. The goal of encouraging tourism by Griffith and Jarratt's Hotel serves as a reminder that the eventual successful protection of the area around the Crater was the result of commercial interests as well as reunions and cultural preservation.[9]

Most visitors to Petersburg and the Crater were interested in walking one of the few remaining sites of the ten-month siege. They toured what was left of the actual crater, gazed at the relics in the museum, but probably did not consider any broader meaning or significance associated with the battle. It is not surprising that within a few short years the veterans of Mahone's Virginia brigade and others would actively engage in remembering and commemorating the battle. William Mahone himself resided in Petersburg, and his involvement in the railroad business and state politics made him a popular, though at times controversial, figure in the community. In addition, the Virginia brigade was made up of regiments formed in the Richmond-Petersburg-Norfolk area, which helped to maintain bonds of esprit de corps throughout the postwar period.

It is also no surprise that the earliest accounts and depictions of the battle struggled to come to terms with the racial dynamic of the engagement at a time when Virginia's political and racial hierarchy were uncertain. The immediate postwar period presented white Southerners with the emotional and psychological effects of defeat as well as the challenge of adjusting to emancipation. Black units remained throughout the South to assist the Freedmen's Bureau in elevating the stature of a newly freed slave population, which numbered roughly 500,000 in Virginia, and worked to enforce the laws of the federal government associated with the Military Reconstruction Acts and Reconstruction Amendments. The presence of black soldiers served as a constant reminder to white Southerners that their antebellum world had been turned upside down.

Edward A. Pollard, who edited the *Daily Richmond Examiner* from 1861 to 1867, wrote one of the earliest postwar accounts of the battle. In *The Lost Cause* (1866), Pollard provided a brief and narrow account of the battle, placing the Virginia brigade of Mahone's division at the center of his narrative. Pollard described the Union attack as feeble until "it was encountered by Mahone's brigade." The racial dynamic of the attack was given prominence, as Mahone's men "were ordered not to fire until they could see the whites of the negroes' eyes." The first volley left these soldiers "panic stricken and past control." Pollard went further in *Southern History of the War,* published in 1866, attributing any appearance of black heroics to the manipulations of "the anti-Slavery party in the North" and arguing that their employment constituted a war crime against the South. Describing black soldiers as pawns of deceitful Northerners enabled Pollard to make the crucial point that without Yankee interference African Americans would have continued to enjoy the peace and comfort of the plantation and would have remained loyal to their white masters. Instead, the former slaves were exposed to the horrors and dangers of the battlefield for reasons unrelated to any concern for their own well-being. Pollard's

The Battle of the Crater by John A. Elder. The painting, commissioned by William Mahone, depicts the men in the Virginia brigade in the countercharge that helped to turn the tide of battle. (Petersburg Museums)

analysis continued a well-rehearsed theme that downplayed the "manly powers" of African Americans in the Union army but also worked to construct a narrative that would come to support and justify the overturning of a racial order imposed by the federal government and a return to power by white Southerners.[10]

Three years later, John Elder—who was present in Petersburg at the time of the battle working as an aide in the field and as a mapmaker—released his dramatic oil painting of the battle, which highlighted the importance of Mahone's counterattack. Elder depicted the fighting at close range in all of its gruesome detail, but the observer's eye is drawn to the advancing tide of Mahone's men in the Twelfth Virginia Infantry, who are poised to sweep the area and put an end to any planned Union advance. One art critic left a colorful review: "The suspense in this portion of the scene is fearful; and one dreads that the reinforcements will arrive to[o] late. But they are hurrying on. With their wild, impulsive yell, so characteristic of the Southern army, regardless of rank or line, in double column, Mahone's brigade comes pouring in." The success of Elder's painting helped to shape the popular belief that Confederate victory could be understood by focusing on the contributions of Virginians.[11]

The release of John Elder's dramatic painting of the Crater in 1869 provided a visual reinforcement of Pollard's description. Any analysis of the racial references in Elder's painting must be understood in the context of the noticeable inroads African Americans were making in state governments throughout the South by the end of the 1860s. Black assertiveness was much more pronounced in the former capital of the Confederacy, as the delegates debated provisions for the disfranchisement of high-ranking rebels, the confiscation of rebel property, the structure of taxation, and the improvement and integration of public facilities. In addition to advancement within the political realm, Virginia's black population openly celebrated Emancipation Day, the Fourth of July, the fall of Richmond (known as Evacuation Day), and the surrender of Robert E. Lee's Army of Northern Virginia. Such public displays served only to remind white Southerners of their subjugation to "Yankee" rule.[12]

The extent to which audiences viewed Elder's painting through a political lens is difficult to gauge. Many, no doubt, simply saw the painting as an attempt to celebrate the heroism of the common soldier. This was the case for the reviewer of one Richmond newspaper, who concluded that Elder had "admirably illustrated that distinguishing trait of the Southern soldier" who "paused not to count the odds, but rushed in forward to the conflict, where death stared him in the face." While other painters concentrated on bringing to life scenes from the war that focused on Confederate generals, this reviewer praised Elder for drawing attention to the "heroism of the private soldier."[13]

At least one reviewer understood Elder's depiction of the Crater as more than praise for the fighting prowess of Mahone's men, describing the artist's purpose as "to rescue from oblivion one scene of our country's glory, and to lift the veil which the conqueror has attempted to cast over our nation's existence, and to show to posterity that, however ultimately defeated, it was only after a struggle worthy of our principles, when our half-starved, emaciated troops, in their tattered uniforms, could in the very jaws of death snatch the victory from the overwhelming numbers opposed to them." By portraying black soldiers along with their "abolitionist" allies as either confused, killed in action, or about to be seriously harmed, Elder delineated a world in sharp distinction to the current and growing racial division within Virginia as the white population was faced with forced social change brought about through black political action. Elder's depiction of Mahone's charge could be interpreted as nothing less than a call to white Virginians to commit themselves to regaining control of the political field, which would be a first step to restructuring the social/racial hierarchy in a way that more closely reflected their antebellum world.[14]

If Elder's painting reflects the bitter resentment and fear whites felt about black political advancement in the immediate postwar period, then the accounts of African American participation at the Crater released in the mid-1870s reflect a more muted and paternalistic tone. The success of Virginia's Conservative Party, which won the governorship and a majority of seats in the general assembly in 1869, and the decision to accept black civil and political equality both guaranteed the franchise for white people and avoided a Republican administration. Conservative victory also opened opportunities for Confederate veterans to commemorate their Lost Cause through public processions that took on a more militaristic form, including uniformed veterans marching with their old colors. All the while Virginians pacified worried Northern onlookers with a language of reconciliation and an olive branch offering to the black population to join the Conservative Party.[15]

Members of the Conservative Party worked to strike the right balance between honoring their Confederate past, containing the fears of Republicans both in the state and up north that the civil rights of African Americans would not be violated, and continuing to reach out to Virginia's black population for its political support. This is most obvious in the decision of Conservative governor James L. Kemper to allow black civic organizations to join in the celebrations surrounding the unveiling of the Stonewall Jackson monument in Capitol Square in Richmond on October 26, 1875. Such a decision reflects the way in which potentially divisive public ceremonies about the late war could be used to demonstrate friendliness toward black people and even gain their political support. Embracing African Americans in such a public way allowed white public officials to showcase a biracial public memory of their Lost Cause. Kemper's position also minimized any political fallout that could be used by Republicans in the next gubernatorial election.[16]

After a ten-year "hibernation," the veterans of the Virginia brigade began to take an active interest in the Crater battlefield. Spurred on by the continued bonds of esprit de corps, veterans used the battlefield to rekindle old friendships as well as to recall the role they had played in securing victory on that day. Compared with casual tourists, these veterans infused the Crater battlefield with a broader meaning and cultural significance, as they acknowledged their commitment to a shared cause that mirrored the growing interest in commemorating the Confederate cause throughout the South.[17]

Interest in the Crater among veterans of the Army of Northern Virginia can be understood on a number of levels. First, the battle was the last decisive victory for Lee's men during the Petersburg campaign. The use of explosives by the Federal army and the destruction they caused left an indelible impression on those present. Most important, the presence of one division of United States Colored Troops brought into sharp relief the distinction between a morally bankrupt Lincoln administration and North and a virtuous South—a binary that was now being emphasized even more in postwar writings.

Confederate veterans from Mahone's Virginia brigade took an active interest in their shared memories, remembering lost comrades and sanctifying their failed attempt at independence, which was still believed to be honorable. The Crater site proved to be an ideal setting for the veterans of Mahone's brigade, who met three times between 1875 and 1877. The first reunion took place in Petersburg on May 10, 1875. Veterans from every regiment traveled to the city to listen to speeches, "see each other face to face, and grasp each other's hands again." J. P. Minetree reminded his audience that those assembled were not simply part of a military organization "that ceased with the surrender at Appomattox Courthouse," but were there to "form an organization to collect the records and preserve the history of our noble brigade, to which we are all so much attached and of which we feel justly proud." Not surprisingly, speeches made direct reference to the Crater, as in the case of Thomas F. Owens, who urged his audience not to forget that "here are the men who hurled back the foe from within a few yards of where we now sit, who had gained possession of our lines by subterranean passage." Close proximity to the old battlefield bestowed the advantage of having the connection between Mahone, his brigade, and the Crater reinforced. The following day thirty-five veterans walked the Crater site with William Mahone.[18]

The men who took part in the first reunion created a "code of organization," the Memorial Association of Mahone's Old Brigade, and voted for officers, including William Mahone as its first president. They also agreed that future reunions should take place on the anniversary of the battle. This decision testifies to the importance of the battle to the identity of the association and guaranteed that memories of the war would be directed or focused on the Crater.

The following July witnessed a more elaborate celebration, which took place in the Opera House of Norfolk, Virginia. Just over 200 veterans traveled to Norfolk for the occasion; on entering the city the veterans were "received with the greatest enthusiasm" as they paraded up Main Street to the Opera House, which was "beautifully decorated." Inside "were scrolls bearing the names of all the principal engagements in which the Brigade had participated." Foreign flags were draped on the walls, and placed prominently on the stage was a Confederate flag presented to one of the regiments during the war. The ceremony got under way with an address by the mayor of Norfolk, John S. Tucker, who welcomed "the heroes of a lost, but glorious cause" and Mahone, "who led these hundreds through our streets" and "the thousands before whose gallant array you rode out so proudly and so worthily, and our hearts were full and our eyes were dimmed."[19]

Focusing on the Crater fight tended to reinforce the overall goals of the reunion, which were, in part, to help veterans deal with the humiliation of defeat and remind them what the common soldier achieved late in the war in the face of the enemy's overwhelming numbers and resources. Speeches made multiple references to the July 30 battle, including Mayor Tucker's; he urged the veterans to remember that "on that day you consummated the full measure of your fame." William Mahone also reminded his men of the "solemn sense of duty which made this day conspicuous in the annals of war, when, by your matchless charge and bayonet, our lines at the Crater were redeemed, and the very safety of our army for the time restored." Toward the end of the ceremony, James B. Hope offered a lengthy "metrical address" that made reference to the Crater:

> Who has forgotten at the deadly Mine
> How our great Captain of great Captains bade
> Your General to retake the captured line?
> How it was done you know, Mahone's Brigade.

Through ceremony, speech, and verse the Crater was no longer a simple tourist attraction but a place where veterans and citizens could honor a

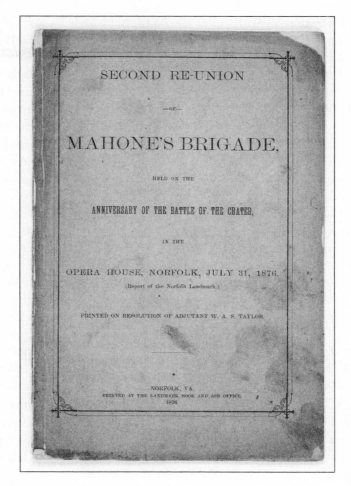

"Second Re-union of Mahone's Brigade" program. Reunions of the veterans of the Virginia brigade served as important rallying points for Mahone's business and political interests. (Virginia Historical Society, Richmond)

glorious past and renew their commitment to prewar Southern values in the face of growing political and social change.[20]

The meeting of the veterans of Mahone's brigade in Norfolk on July 31, 1876, can be seen as an attempt to honor the Confederate cause without upsetting the local black population or giving Republicans reason to wave the "bloody shirt." Veterans marched in uniform and as members of individual regiments with colors displayed, banners with the names of individual regiments and battles decorated the walls of the hall, and a Confederate flag graced center stage. Meeting on the anniversary of the battle of the Crater attests to the importance Mahone's men attached to it and no doubt reminded many of the veterans of their horror at having had to fight black Union soldiers just twelve years earlier. Absent from the ceremony, however, were any references to the presence of African Americans in the battle. Organizers of the reunion remained focused on honoring the heroism of the Confederate soldier and remembering the fallen: "We miss their familiar forms—some of them were our brothers—*all of them died for us.*"[21]

Though the organizers of the reunion of Mahone's brigade chose to steer clear of any direct references to the presence of black soldiers at the Crater, individual accounts of the battle continued to do so, but in a way that reflected changing political boundaries. In November of that same year, at a meeting of the Association of the Army of Northern Virginia, Captain W. Gordon McCabe presented a detailed account of the Crater, which was reprinted in the *Southern Historical Society Papers.* McCabe had served as an adjutant in Pegram's Battalion of Artillery and had been present during the Crater fight. His account highlighted the construction of the mine and offered exhaustive coverage of the movements of individual units, starting with the initial Union assault and ending with the final charge of Sanders's Alabama brigade. In all of this, McCabe made only passing reference to the "drunken battalions of Ferrero." McCabe was convinced that the black soldiers were "inflamed with drink." What is striking in McCabe's account is the absence of old feelings of anger and hatred or the way in which the presence of African American soldiers served to rally Confederates both during the battle and in the following weeks. References to intoxicated black soldiers reinforced the belief that unless the African American community was agitated, it would remain peaceful and subservient to white Virginians.[22]

More revealing of political currents in Virginia is the account by William Stewart, who commanded the Sixty-first Virginia. Stewart almost entirely ignored how Confederates felt upon learning of their colored adversaries. After twelve years the feelings of outrage, fear, and hatred were absent from the few references Stewart made regarding their performance. Stewart recalled that the black soldiers begged for their lives and "were victims of an uncontrollable terror." According to Stewart, one cried out,

"I nebber pinted a gun at a white man in all my life; dem nasty stinking Yankees" were to blame. The day after the battle, Stewart remembered, he encountered a "negro between the lines, who had both legs blown off. . . . Some of our men managed to shove a cup of water to him, which he drank, and immediately commenced frothing at the mouth, and died in a very short time afterwards." It is no accident that Stewart selectively conveyed two stories that addressed in a post-emancipation world the desire to maintain antebellum notions of racial hierarchy. Not only were black men not interested in fighting for their freedom, but even after a bloody battle white Southerners' sense of paternalism could still be exercised. Stewart makes no reference to the massacres of black soldiers mentioned in Confederate wartime accounts. Stewart's account betrays a firm belief in the inferiority of black soldiers and in the folly of Union officers who believed that black troops could contribute to a successful operation. In addition, Stewart's decision to close his account with the description of an act of kindness toward a seriously wounded black soldier suggests that he wanted to emphasize the possibility of cooperation between the races at a time when the Conservative Party continued to exercise political control in Virginia.[23]

No one loomed larger over the burgeoning memory of the battle of the Crater than William Mahone. The son of innkeepers, William Mahone was born in Southampton County, Virginia, on December 1, 1826. Mahone's interest in railroads and engineering was nurtured while he was a cadet at the Virginia Military Institute between 1844 and 1847. Later he advanced rapidly with the Orange and Alexandria Railroad, Fredericksburg and Valley Plank Road, and finally, by 1853, as chief engineer of the Norfolk and Petersburg Railroad. On the eve of Virginia's secession, Mahone served also as the railroad's president and superintendent.[24]

Mahone responded enthusiastically to Virginia's ordinance of secession in April 1861. Though he rose steadily through the ranks, from colonel of the Sixth Virginia Infantry to the rank of brigadier general, he failed to distinguish himself in any of the major battles from Manassas to Gettysburg and on more than one occasion he was sharply rebuked by superiors. It was not until the beginning of Ulysses S. Grant's Overland Campaign in May 1864 that Mahone demonstrated strong leadership qualities. His brigade fought well at the Wilderness, and he was given command of a division (including his old Virginia brigade) after Longstreet's wounding and the necessary reshuffling of commands. He took his division into the maelstroms of Spotsylvania and Cold Harbor before returning to Petersburg, the center of his business interests. It was due to his performance at the Crater that Mahone was finally promoted to the rank of major general. Throughout the final nine months of the war, Mahone and his division fought in many of the battles around Petersburg before surrendering one of the largest intact units at Appomattox.[25]

After the war "the Hero of the Crater" returned home to Petersburg and to the railroad business, where he continued to flourish. By 1867 Mahone was president of three railroads in Virginia, which he hoped to consolidate into one line. To achieve these goals, Mahone offered financial support to Virginia's anti-Reconstruction Conservative Party, or "Bourbons," and moderate Republicans, which led to the end of Reconstruction in 1869. Mahone also supported Gilbert C. Walker in 1869 and James Kemper in 1873 for governor in exchange for their support of consolidation. That support resulted in the creation of the Atlantic, Mississippi, and Ohio Railroad in 1870 and Mahone's election as president with a salary of $25,000.

Mahone's consolidation program, however, was not without its critics. Residents of Alexandria, Lynchburg, and Richmond worried about the possible economic pitfalls related to consolidation, such as decreased trade as well as relative freedom of trade. Many simply concluded that Mahone was motivated by self-interest and that the potential for a monopoly was not in the state's interests. One observer opined that Mahone was "the most overrated railroad man in Virginia" and went on to note disappointedly that the advocates of consolidation "seem to have concluded that he is the only man living who can make the scheme a success."[26]

Meanwhile, Mahone understood that to gain and maintain sufficient support in the halls of the state legislature and in the community at large he would have to construct a public image that could reassure his constituency of his sincere motives and of the prospect of prosperity for the state through the economic changes connected to consolidation. One close business associate, Abram Fulkerson, warned Mahone that Virginia was "averse to jumping into new movements, in other words she abhors innovations." There is no direct evidence that Mahone engaged in a comprehensive campaign to promote—or embellish—his war record with the intention of furthering his business interests. It can be surmised, however, that Mahone acknowledged on some level that a public image based on his service to the Confederacy would have positive effects. Newspapers in support of Mahone's business plans took the lead in citing the general's war record. "Had our late war continued several years longer," asserted one commentator in December 1868, "we do not doubt that General Mahone would have been one of the leaders of our Southern struggle." Luckily for Mahone, his performance at the Crater in July 1864 could easily be billed as a courageous defense of the residents of Petersburg, Richmond, and the rest of Virginia.[27]

The release of John Elder's painting of the Crater and its emphasis on the Virginia brigade constituted an important public relations victory for Mahone in the Richmond-Petersburg area on the eve of the consolidation vote by the state legislature. On July 4 of that year, Mahone was praised at the Virginia Military Institute in a memorial poem for "Stonewall" Jackson read by James Barron Hope. Hope compared Mahone to Jackson and referred to both Elder's painting of the Crater and a recent bust of Mahone sculpted by Edward Valentine. The ceremony was accompanied by the unveiling of "portraits of the alumni of the Institute who fell in battle" as well as five "portraits of those still living"—Mahone being one of the five. Around the same time, Mahone became active in veterans affairs by serving as Virginia's representative to the Confederate Burial and Memorial Association, whose purpose was to reinter the remains of those who had died in battles throughout the South "and to make arrangements to erect at some place . . . a monument to their memory."[28]

More far-reaching was the publication of an authorized biography of Mahone's military career written by John Watts De Peyster—himself a general in the New York militia—which was published in the *New York Historical Magazine* in June 1870. It is unclear how the two met and difficult to piece together why a former Confederate general and Virginia businessman would seek publicity in New York. Mahone may have seen the publication of a biographical sketch in a popular Northern publication as a way to attract additional investments for his newly consolidated railroad. With the final approval of consolidation, Mahone desperately needed to sell bonds for the new railroad, and the pool of potential Northern investors, according to one of Mahone's correspondents, constituted "an advantage we should not ignore."[29]

The De Peyster sketch served Mahone's business interests in a number of ways, most notably by representing him as an early point of reconciliation between North and South: "Ability, however and wherever displayed in an eminent degree, is the property of our common country; and no man between the oceans, the gulf, and the lakes, is a finer illustration of the innate military capacity and adaptability of the American people than the subject of this sketch." De Peyster described Mahone as "audacious," "enterprising," and "aggressive"—all qualities that might attract potential investors.[30]

Not surprisingly, Mahone's conduct at the "Crater fight" provided De Peyster the opportunity to present an account that blended all of these qualities. The author leaves little doubt as to who was responsible for throwing back the Union assault. According to De Peyster, "the whole credit of our [Union] repulse belongs to him," and he goes on to suggest that "we could have gone straight into Petersburg, but for the timely appearance of the Civil Engineer and natural General Mahone." "Mahone's promptness and audacity," concludes De Peyster, "should immortalize him."[31]

Lastly, while Mahone's participation in the reunions of the Virginia brigade offered him a chance to renew old relationships, it also worked to highlight his war record at a time when his public reputation was coming under increasing pressure. The first meeting, held in Petersburg, attests to the importance of Mahone in the organization of the group's identity. Initial calls for the reunion were arranged under the name of David Weisiger, who led the brigade after Mahone's promotion to division command. Numerous newspaper editorials, including the *Norfolk Virginian,* called for a change in name since Weisiger commanded the brigade only during the last phase of the war. The *Virginia Sentinel* urged the association: "By all means let them bear the name by which they won so many honors and gained undying fame as 'Mahone's Brigade.'" Mahone surely made this transition more likely with his decision to offer "a special rate" for the roughly 200 veterans to make the passage on his railroad lines to Petersburg.[32]

It was the second reunion of Mahone's Old Brigade, taking place in the Norfolk Opera House in 1876 on the anniversary of the battle of the Crater, that provided Mahone with a unique opportunity to deliver his speech, which forged a bond of bravery, sacrifice, and service between those killed during the war and its survivors: "It is to commemorate the historic estate which belongs to you and to their memories, to yours and to theirs, and to enter it of record, that constitutes now your duty and the sacred purposes of your organization." In addition, James Hope—the editor of the Norfolk *Landmark*—and William Cameron both followed Mahone with addresses that once again placed him at the center of the Confederate pantheon.[33]

It would be a mistake to interpret these reunions simply as opportunities for Mahone and the veterans of his old brigade to come together to share memories of fallen comrades and commemorate their "Lost Cause." Though busy with the continuing financial crisis plaguing his railroad, in the weeks leading up to all three reunions, Mahone kept abreast of developments and may have exerted influence on the decision to change the name of the organization. Many of the association's officers were close business associates and future political allies of Mahone, and in the 1880s the general kept a ledger containing the names of survivors of the organization. Close contact with the veterans that served in the five regiments of the old Virginia brigade—all raised in the Richmond-Petersburg-Norfolk area—along with the reunions constituted an opportunity through public address to present Mahone as an ally of Virginia's interests by reminding the Commonwealth of his service in the war. The veterans themselves could be counted on as foot soldiers to further his growing political aspirations. Indeed, the third reunion of the brigade took place on the anniversary of the Crater in 1877, only a few days before the Conservative convention that was to decide on a gubernatorial candidate, of which Mahone was one.[34]

In the fifteen years following the end of the war, the Crater battlefield witnessed a steady stream of attention, from visitors looking for physical traces of war to the veterans of the Virginia brigade who gathered to rekindle old friendships and recall acts of heroism on the site of one of the last dramatic Confederate victories in Virginia. Throughout these fifteen years, written and visual accounts of the battle acknowledged the outrage associated with the presence of black Union soldiers, but they did so in a way that reflected the reality of emancipation and changing racial boundaries. With few exceptions, early postwar accounts treated this racial dimension of the battle in a way that reinforced a return to home rule after 1870 as well as deeply ingrained assumptions about the fighting prowess of African Americans. Finally, William Mahone utilized his war record and fame as the "Hero of the Crater" to advance both his business and political interests at a time when black Virginians remained potential supporters in both realms.

Chapter 3

VIRGINIA'S RECONSTRUCTION

William Mahone, "Hero of the Crater"

LESS THAN TWO weeks before a scheduled reunion of the Third Georgia Regiment in August 1883, Robert Bagby—who had served in Company H—was "surprised" to read in a local newspaper an editorial from a fellow veteran "objecting" to the proposed presence of their former commander, Major General William Mahone. Bagby's response indicates that he understood the origin of this complaint. He assured his comrade that "the men who are invited to meet us on this occasion are expected to do so as survivors of a Lost Cause and not as representatives of a State or Federal Politics." The distinction drawn between the acknowledgment of a shared Confederate past and more recent political alignments reflects the extent to which Mahone's war record had become clouded by his foray into Virginia and national politics. Bagby assured his readers that he did not necessarily approve of Mahone's politics but was convinced that he could welcome his former commander with open arms: "It is not my wish or desire to applaud Gen. Mahone for the active part he bore in the late war between the States, or vilify or abuse him for his connection with Virginia politics but as a Confederate soldier who followed where he led in the dark and trying hours of the past. I, for one, am willing to let politics of the living present rest long enough to remember the record made by Gen. Mahone while fighting for a principle that was near and dear to us all."[1]

By 1883, William Mahone had become one of the most controversial and divisive politicians in the country. As the organizer and leader of the Readjuster Party (named for its policy of downwardly "readjusting" Virginia's state debt), Mahone led the most successful independent coalition of black and white Republicans and white Democrats. From 1879 to 1883,

Postwar image of William Mahone. (Library of Congress, Washington, D.C.)

Readjusters governed the state. They elected a governor and two U.S. senators and served in six of Virginia's ten congressional districts. With Mahone at the helm of the party and buttressed by Senate patronage, the coalition controlled the state legislature and the courts. As a result, a large percentage of the state's federal offices went to the Readjusters' black majority. These African Americans played a prominent role in shaping the party's platform, which resulted in their gaining increased access to the polls, officeholding, and jury service.

The legislative agenda of the Readjusters, as well as Mahone's prominent role within the party and the U.S. Senate, generated heated attacks in newspapers and more personal forms of communication. Even the duel, which had disappeared from the South during the first two decades after the Civil War, reappeared during the four years of Readjuster control. Like former Confederate general James Longstreet, Mahone incurred the wrath of a growing and influential Lost Cause movement that, in addition to rationalizing Confederate defeat, sought to maintain Democratic Party solidarity by fostering white supremacy and states' rights. Though Longstreet's affiliation with the Republican Party resulted in his being blamed not only for Confederate defeat at Gettysburg but for the loss of the war as well, Mahone's postwar political career presented conservative Virginians with a more immediate threat. Lost Cause advocates continually attacked Mahone and the Readjusters because the increased involvement of African Americans in the political process constituted a direct threat to their goal of turning back the clock to a point in the prewar past when white Southern slaveholders stood atop the social and political hierarchy.[2]

Lost Cause advocates such as Jubal Early and others assumed an aggressive posture against Mahone and other former Confederates who threatened their own conservative social and political agenda. That Mahone was not an outsider but a popular Confederate major general meant that he had to be dealt with severely, and they responded in large part by attacking his war record. His detractors assailed a war record that Mahone and his close associates helped construct—and often embellished—to further his own postwar career, first as a railroad magnate, next as an unsuccessful candidate for the 1877 gubernatorial nomination, and finally as a leader of the Readjusters and U.S. senator aligned with the Republican Party.

A closer look at Mahone's postwar difficulties sheds light on the heated debates, or "reputation war," surrounding the political limits to which the Confederate past could be applied. A more careful examination will also undermine the notion that Southerners—especially Virginians—were in agreement over who could claim rightful ownership of their past. Although historians have shown the influence of sectional reconciliation and other conditions on early histories of the war, they have not examined sufficiently the extent to which Virginians fought over the conditions under which one could claim a legitimate connection to the Confederate past. In this case the heated disputes reached into and even divided the small community of veterans that Mahone helped to maintain through the 1870s.[3]

Mahone's plunge into Virginia politics and unsuccessful bid for the gubernatorial nomination followed quickly on the heels of the loss of the Atlantic, Mississippi, and Ohio railroad to receivership in 1876. The issue that propelled Mahone into the political arena was the question of what to do about the state's debt. By 1870 it had amounted to $45 million—much of it having been incurred before the war, when Virginia was committed to internal improvements and when its boundaries included the new state of West Virginia. The issue was necessarily divisive because it directly affected the state's revenue and previous legislation that had authorized financial support for the fledgling public school system and other social services. Although Mahone made it clear that the debt could not be ignored entirely, in June 1877 he went on record as a "friend of the public school system of Virginia," which he believed "should be effectually nurtured." In readjusting the debt downward, Mahone believed there would be enough left to finance the public schools. In 1877 he organized a faction with the Conservative Democratic Party supporting readjustment while contesting the gubernatorial nomination. Unable to win a majority of the delegates to the party's convention, Mahone released his supporters, leading to the nomination and election of Frederick Holliday.[4]

Only after Governor Holliday had, in early 1879, vetoed a measure to reduce the debt and redirected funds appropriated for the public schools to help pay the interest on the debt did Mahone split from the Conservative Party and call a convention of self-styled "Readjusters." The division between Readjusters and their opponents was drawn along racial, social, and political lines. Much of the early support for readjustment came from poor whites in western counties and prosperous yeoman farmers in the Shenandoah Valley, who were enthusiastic about the benefits of public schools and resentful of the more conservative counties in eastern Virginia. White and black urban workers and agricultural workers also supported readjustment. Members of Virginia's black population—many committed to the Republican Party—argued that since they had played no part in contracting the debt during the antebellum years, they were not responsible. Those advocating paying off the debt in its entirety, called "Funders," tended to be the more conservative elements in the state, including bankers and large businessmen, residents of more urban centers, and white men living in counties dominated by African Americans. The choice for some Funders was not a mutually exclusive one but a question of what deserved priority. In short, paying off the debt was a matter of honor.[5]

Once organized, the Readjusters placed William Cameron, veteran of the Twelfth Virginia Infantry, in the governor's mansion and won election in six of Virginia's ten congressional districts. With a majority of Readjusters in the General Assembly, Mahone was elected to the U.S. Senate, slated to take his seat in March 1881.

The success of the Readjusters was based in part on their ability to reach voters who had been excluded or previously ignored in political matters. This achievement galvanized Virginia's black population with the possibility of increased participation in politics. At the same time, the success of Mahone and the Readjusters concerned those Virginians who worried about any political, racial, and social realignment. Such realignments during this period, and their accompanying debates, were arguably the most heated since the brief period leading to Virginia's secession back in April 1861. In 1880 a pamphlet appeared: *John Brown and William Mahone: An Historical Parallel, Foreshadowing Civil Trouble,* by George W. Bagby. "In 1858 occurred the raid of John Brown," wrote Bagby, misdating the 1859 incident at Harpers Ferry. The "raid" of Mahone and the Readjusters in 1879, though "less bloody," was "more dangerous than that of John Brown." "Both raids occurred in Va, and the negro was in both cases the instrument relied on to destroy the old order of things." Linking Mahone and Brown accomplished a number of goals. First, memories of John Brown could easily be recalled because of the visceral fears that his actions had engendered. It also made clear the extent of the current perceived threat to the stability of the Commonwealth and at the same time called Mahone's loyalty into question.[6]

Around the same time an editorial in the *Richmond Times* suggested that the Readjuster Party constituted "one of the nastiest and most infamous governments" and that "General Mahone was instigator and mainspring of every act in that government that humiliated Virginians." Along with calling into question the nature of Readjuster rule, emphasizing Mahone's military background with the title "General" helped bring to light concerns about his "sincerity" and, perhaps more important, his "patriotism."[7]

Throughout the four years of Readjuster control, both sides focused on Mahone's war record. To his supporters, Mahone's service to the Confederacy reflected not only commitment to independence but also to the welfare of the Commonwealth. Mahone's enemies attacked his war record and military reputation with the ultimate goal of challenging his loyalty to the Lost Cause as well as his interest in the continued welfare of the state. At least one Mahone supporter acknowledged the close connection being drawn between the politics of debt and the Confederate past: "Frequently we hear appeals to the late Confederate soldiers to maintain the honor and credit of old Virginia now as they were wont to do at such perils and sacrifices as characterized them from Manassas to Appomattox. Lately we saw it stated that nearly all the Generals of Virginia were funders and therefore the soldiers should be." A writer with the *Southern Intelligencer* concluded that Mahone "does not care enough for what Lee and Jackson would have done [about the state debt] if they were now alive."[8]

Mahone's supporters no doubt found it easy to connect his political goals with his military career by building on an interpretation contained in the De Peyster sketch as well as Mahone's own activities with Confederate veterans and, most important, the general's proximity to the old Crater battlefield. One Virginia newspaper claimed that Mahone displayed "the very highest qualities of the born soldier," and his "tenacity, dash, and skill" never failed "to inspire confidence in him and dismay in the enemy's army." Another Virginian took issue with a statement made by former Confederate general Joseph Johnston, who called Mahone one of "the finest specimens of a newspaper General." The writer responded: "The truth is there was no officer in the Army of Northern Virginia whose reputation rested more exclusively upon his own individual merits than William Mahone." Even readers in the remote state of Iowa were informed that Mahone's "line was the last to give way at Appomattox. He was among the most trusted soldiers in the confederacy, and ranked with Longstreet and Pickett as a fighting commander who always led his men." The *Norfolk Landmark* anticipated "that the time will come when Virginia will do him [Mahone] honor as the hero of the Crater," because it was he who on that occasion "saved Lee's army."[9]

More than one newspaper repeated a widely accepted story originating with J. Horace Lacy that toward the end of the war Lee had Mahone in mind to replace him in the event of his death or inability to continue to lead the army. "There is little doubt," according to the *Capital*, "if in the last year of the war General Lee had been killed, disabled or removed from causes unforeseen from the head of the army, that Mahone would have

This postwar view of the Crater was produced for Union veterans on a tour of Civil War battlefields, probably in the 1880s. (Virginia Historical Society, Richmond)

taken his place." Another writer followed De Peyster's sketch closely, acknowledging that Mahone's "division laid down more muskets" at Appomattox "than any other one in the army." "It was the recognition of these qualities in the military character of Mahone," continued the writer, "which impelled Lee to name him as the Commander-in-Chief of the Confederacy when he expected to retire." Regardless of the story's popularity, there is no wartime evidence to confirm that Lee intended to place Mahone in command of the army. The widespread use of Mahone's war record and the tendency to exaggerate his importance throughout the war only fueled the anger of his political enemies.[10]

In November 1881 Readjusters capitalized on their gains when they elected William Cameron to the governor's chair and elected H. H. Riddleberger to join Mahone in the Senate. Mahone himself took his seat in March of that year at a time when the Senate was evenly divided between Republicans and Democrats. If Mahone's loyalty to Virginia and the

South had been questioned because of the legislative agenda of the Read-justers, his decision to cast his vote with the South's old political enemy could be interpreted as nothing less than apostasy. With Mahone's sup-port, the Republican Party was able to organize the Senate around its own legislative goals. As a reward for his support, Mahone was given the chair-manship of the Committee on Agriculture as well as membership on three additional committees. More important, Mahone gained the support of the federal administration in the form of an extensive patronage, which allowed him to advance the careers of African American supporters in Washington and Virginia.[11]

With Readjusters in control of both houses of the state legislature and Cameron in the governor's chair, legislation was easily passed. The state debt was readjusted downward to $21 million, which left sufficient funds for public schools, the hiring of black teachers, and even a hospital for mentally ill African Americans. Readjusters abolished the poll tax, which had been used to disfranchise black voters, and the whipping post. In 1882 the General Assembly passed legislation supporting the literacy fund with an appropriation of $379,270, plus an additional payment to public schools; schools with black teachers were also given support. The sum of $100,000 was appropriated to support the founding of the Normal and Collegiate Institute (later Virginia State University) and Central Hospital in Petersburg, both for African Americans. Readjusters also cut property taxes for poor farmers by 20 percent.[12]

Black Virginians were rewarded for their votes on both the state and federal levels through political patronage. The presence of African Ameri-cans increased sharply in different agencies, including the Treasury De-partment, Pensions Bureau, Secretary's Office, and Interior Department. At the height of Readjuster control, African Americans made up 38 per-cent of workers in the post office. With Mahone's help, African Americans also found jobs as clerks and copyists in Washington. It was in the field of education, however, where blacks enjoyed the most visible increase in participation. Readjuster reforms increased the number of black teachers from 415 in 1879 to 1,588 in 1884, and black student enrollment went from 36,000 to 91,000 during those years. In addition, African Ameri-cans served as jurors and clerks, policemen in towns, and guards at state penitentiaries.[13]

Although black Virginians were integral to the Readjuster Party's continued success, the irony of a former Confederate general actively courting their vote did not go unnoticed. "Those who had been the bitter-est and most dangerous foes to the Colored People," wrote the biographer of black Readjuster Robert A. Paul, "were calling for their support. . . . The one who had hurled hundreds of colored soldiers into the death-fraught crater of Petersburg had announced himself the leader and direc-tor of the new party. They who had fought on the field of blood and labored in the arena of politics to deprive the Colored man of his consti-tutional rights now proclaimed that Colored men should enjoy the full rights and prerogatives of citizens."[14]

Attacks against Mahone increased in number and intensity as Read-juster legislation and Mahone's influence in the Senate brought to the forefront groups that had been barred from any serious participation in both state and local government. For Virginia's more conservative citizens, such changes were seen as a threat to the stability of what they perceived to be established social hierarchies. Reporters covering debates on the floor of the Senate noted, "Southern Senators speak as bitterly of General Mahone and his followers as they did of carpet-baggers, scalawags, and niggers." The *Richmond State* urged its readers to stand guard against "the treason of many of [Virginia's] own sons who in times past were counted among her most devoted and loyal defenders and protectors." Without mentioning Mahone by name, the editor reminded his readers, "The Revolution gave us but one ARNOLD, during the whole seven years of its course, while the Confederate war failed to yield a single one on either side until after it had been fought out." Though many of Virginia's native sons "held out long and well . . . at last some of them succumbed, and are now found, ARNOLD-like, leading their old enemy against their old friends and associates." Earlier comparisons with John Brown had emphasized the perceived threat to the political and social structure that Mahone and the Readjusters represented, but comparisons with Benedict Arnold reinforced the belief that Mahone had betrayed his fellow Virginians, including for-mer Confederates, for political and economic gain.[15]

On the eve of the 1881 gubernatorial election, Mahone and Jubal Early—now associated with the Funders—rekindled an old feud that had originated following the publication of the De Peyster sketch back in 1870. Furious with the way he was portrayed in that publication, Early initiated a monthlong correspondence with Mahone that almost resulted in a duel. According to De Peyster, "Although his name was Early, he was always late. Jubal was always hesitating whether to fight or not; he would ride up and down the lines, from fifteen to twenty minutes, debating whether or not to begin; whereas the battle was to be won or lost meanwhile." Rumors of a duel to be fought intensified and broadened the rift between the two former Confederates. Finally, in October 1881, Early published the entire correspondence. The pamphlet numbered nineteen pages, including comments by Early, and was sent to newspapers for reprinting. The publication of the correspondence gave Early the last word on the subject. However, the importance of its publication lies in the fact that it opened an avenue of attack that connected Mahone's political career with his identity as a former Confederate officer.[16]

Such a connection was easily inferred by observers. "The fate of Southern generals, no matter how brilliant their career during the war, who have ventured since the peace to entertain opinions disagreeable to their fellow citizens . . . is not a pleasant one." Comparing Mahone with both James Longstreet and John Mosby, this particular commentator stated confidently that as "long as he remained in sympathy with the Bourbons he was the darling of the Southern Democracy," but as soon as he strayed from accepted discourse, he "found himself an outlaw and held up to scorn." The emotionalism of such attacks surpassed those leveled at Longstreet and Mosby because of the nature of the changes taking place in Virginia, Mahone's alliance with the Republican Party, and the possibility that Readjuster success might serve as a catalyst for independent movements elsewhere. At least one writer wondered "who shall be selected as the Mahone of Georgia politics." In addition to Georgia, between 1880 and 1884 independent candidates and movements were launched in Mississippi, North Carolina, and Texas.[17]

Funder-supported organs also challenged Mahone's loyalty to the men who had served under him in the war. Such a move countered the steps Mahone himself had taken after the war to enlist their support for his business interests and political aspirations—most notably through the reunions of "Mahone's Brigade Association." One newspaper accused Mahone and the Readjusters of removing "gallant, disabled soldiers" from public positions "and putting in their places negroes, who have no claims upon the State." Mahone's detractors not only attacked the growing involvement of black Readjusters in positions of power but also helped paint Mahone as a betrayer of former comrades and the Confederate cause. "When a Confederate soldier so far forgets the memories of the lost cause, as to displace fellow comrades who lost their limbs in battling for that cause," mused one newspaper editorial, "he is not likely to hesitate to go further for party purposes." Mahone's enemies also challenged his loyalty to his former comrades with broadsides. One such example announced in bold letters, "CONFEDERATE SOLDIERS DEPRIVED OF BREAD BY MAHONE."[18]

It is difficult to gauge the extent of the damage to the bond that Mahone had worked to establish with his fellow veterans. Funder attacks reflect the fact that Confederate veterans were now being perceived as a highly politicized group whose loyalty to former commanders could be trumped by political concerns. Presenting a united front, veterans of Mahone's Virginia brigade rallied in defense of their former commander. "General Mahone has shown us a way out of the woods," asserted one veteran, and "we shall follow him and fear no danger." Another former soldier, writing under the pen name Private True and aiming to show that Mahone and the Readjuster Party had not betrayed Virginia's veterans, exclaimed that the highest officers within the Readjuster Party, including Senator Riddleberger, Congressman John Paul, Governor "Willie" Cameron, and Secretary of State William Elam had all either been privates in the war or had risen in the ranks to first lieutenant.[19]

Not surprisingly, the most common target for Mahone's political enemies was his performance at the Crater. As has already been demonstrated, Mahone had built his postwar reputation around the leadership qualities he displayed on that battlefield, which many argued had been responsible for the Confederate victory. His performance on that day was a central focus of most biographical accounts, including De Peyster's, and the memories of many of the veterans of Mahone's Virginia brigade hinged on the assumption that their old leader had performed admirably. In addition, the Crater proved to be an ideal target because of its continued popularity as a point of curiosity for Virginians as well as a site for the reunion of Northern veterans. In reference to the Crater, many of Mahone's detractors questioned his conduct on the battlefield, whether he had ordered the charge that led to the retaking of the salient, and whether he in fact had led his old brigade in its recapture.[20]

The most significant challenge to Mahone's conduct at the Crater came from his former subordinate Brigadier General David A. Weisiger, who took command of the Virginia brigade following Mahone's promotion to division command. In June 1880 the Funder-supported *Richmond Commonwealth* reprinted a letter sent by Weisiger to Captain Gordon McCabe asserting that Mahone never left the safety of the "covered way," which the brigade used for shelter before the final push to retake a portion of the Crater, and that he selected the position from which the brigade would attack. In addition to claiming that Mahone had shirked his duty for the safety of cover, in September 1880 Weisiger wrote in the *Richmond State* that he himself "gave the order to 'forward!' at the opportune moment, when it was observed that the enemy were preparing for a charge."[21]

Mahone's defenders were quick to respond to these challenges. Four former members of the Virginia brigade collected nineteen accounts from fellow veterans of the unit, all of which challenged specific points made by Weisiger. About half of these accounts were penned before the political upheaval associated with Readjuster control. Their accounts were prefaced by the acknowledgment that "events have occurred since" the battle "that have separated the actors in that scene. . . . But, whenever the members of that heroic Old Brigade revert to the Crater fight, it stands before them distinct and vivid as in the hour it was waged." In presenting a unified front, Mahone's supporters hoped to put to rest any doubt concerning his performance at the Crater.[22]

Lieutenant John Laughton of the Twelfth Virginia recalled having "seen Gen. Mahone superintending the formation of the line," as did William Coldwell, who remembered that he "overtook Gen. Mahone and an engineer officer" as they moved along the covered way into position. Coldwell made it a point to acknowledge that though he was not a "political friend" of Mahone's, he could not stand by and allow his reputation to be "traduced and vilified by the envy, hatred and malice of enemies, fifteen years after Robert E. Lee acknowledged his just glory by promoting him." "Gen. Mahone was in the trenches before and after the final charge," according to Colonel George T. Rogers of the Sixth Virginia, "and directed each action of the brigade . . . during the greater part of that terrible battle, as he did the movements of each other brigade engaged." James Blakemore placed Mahone a "short distance from and a little in advance of the left of the line of our formation and who was then awaiting the movements of Georgia brigade, emerging from the covered way." Mahone's men also took issue with Weisiger's claim that it was he who gave the order to attack. For the eight men of Companies A and B of the Sixteenth Virginia, Mahone's role was solidified in their collective memories: "Contrary to this assumption on Gen. Weisiger's part, we feel perfectly free to say that Gen. Mahone was with his Old Brigade, and that we know he superintended the arranging of the troops in line of battle; that we saw him pass down the line, and heard him give the command, 'Fix bayonets! Reserve your fire until you get to the breastworks!'"[23]

Readjuster-backed organs such as the *Virginian* also fired back in defense of Mahone. H. H. Riddleberger countered by pointing out the connection between politics and the attacks on Mahone's reputation by Funder-backed newspapers; he went on to defend Mahone by urging readers to remember that the "old veterans of his famous command . . . still hurrah for Mahone." In addition, reference to Lee's own ability to "judge" the "courage" and "qualifications of his subordinates" aided Mahone's defense. Finally, it was hoped that remembering that Lee "would have elected between Mahone and [John B.] Gordon" to replace him as commander of the Army of Northern Virginia, if necessary, would provide a final vindication for Mahone.[24]

In a letter to the editor of the *Richmond Times,* Charles S. Venable, who had served on Lee's staff, commented on recently reprinted accounts of the battle of the Crater that he believed made an "exceedingly false impression in regard to General Mahone and his superb conduct on that occasion." Venable countered by reassuring the editor that "every message sent that day by General Lee (who was near by), was sent to Gen. Mahone, as commander of the troops engaged [in] repelling the enemy at the Crater and the adjacent line."[25]

The continued attacks on Mahone's war record and the spirited defenses of it reflect the importance that both sides attached to the Confederate past, and specifically the Crater. No doubt the confused nature of the fighting in and around the Crater made it possible to draw conflicting conclusions surrounding central questions related to the battle. Arguably, the truth of what happened at the Crater was the least important concern for the participants in the ongoing debates. Neither side was interested in forging a mutually agreed-upon account of what happened at the Crater because they both were content simply to make political use of their disparate memories.

In November 1883 Readjuster control of Virginia ended abruptly as a result of a race riot in Danville, which left one white man and four black men dead just three days before the state elections. Democrats seized on the riot as evidence of the fruits of Readjuster legislation and capitalized on it by winning two-thirds of the seats in both branches of the General Assembly. Mahone's control of the state government was broken. In 1884 the situation deteriorated further when Mahone decided to campaign for

James G. Blaine in the presidential election under the banner of the Republican Party. Grover Cleveland won the state by 6,000 votes, as Democrats in the state legislature continued to replace Republican and Readjuster officeholders.[26]

Replacement of Readjuster officials proceeded aggressively. A Virginia newspaper assured its readers that "the good work will surely go on until not one single Mahoneite is left in office." Outside Virginia, observers predicted that with Cleveland's victory, "he will fling all civil service reform professions to the winds and set up the guillotine until the head of every friend of General Mahone has dropped into the basket." Such editorials attest not only to popular perception of Mahone's position as leader of the Readjusters but also to the belief that he alone was responsible for the radical political and social changes that took place in Virginia.[27]

Finally, with Fitzhugh Lee's ascendancy to the governorship in 1885 and Democratic control of the state legislature, Mahone's service in the U.S. Senate was terminated. Fitzhugh Lee and the Democrats' success in the gubernatorial election of 1885 hinged in part on the party's ability to appropriate much of the Readjusters' legislative program, including free school textbooks, public education, and Virginia's first comprehensive pension scheme for Confederate veterans. Lee may also have taken a page out of Mahone's political handbook by presenting himself as a war hero. It was not uncommon for Lee to enter a town with a military escort. While campaigning through Rockbridge County, "he was mounted on a magnificent bay horse, and looked as he rode through the crowded streets every inch a soldier," remembered one observer. Stories also abounded citing Lee's deliberate invocation of his famous uncle, Robert E. Lee; he used the Confederate hero's saddle during his tour of Virginia's western counties. Lee also employed a "headquarters stand of colors used by Gen. Geo. E. Pickett," which accompanied the "mounted men that escorted the gallant cavalier in his movements through the country."[28]

Mahone remained loyal to the Republican Party until he died in 1895, though he was never able to achieve the kind of victory won by the Readjusters. Nevertheless, his work to defeat the Bourbons and further the interests of Virginia's African American population led on occasion to impressive results. In 1886 Republicans captured seven of the ten congressional seats in Virginia, and in the presidential canvass that followed in 1888, Mahone brought the Republicans to within 1,500 votes of victory. As he did with the Readjusters, Mahone kept tight control of the Republican political machine. Reactions to his close oversight of affairs ranged from accusations of dictatorial control to the abandonment of the Republican Party for personal as well as ideological and political disagreements. Finally, in 1889 Mahone ran unsuccessfully for governor by campaigning on behalf of a protective tariff that he hoped would aid Virginia's industrial workers.[29]

Throughout this period, Mahone was forced to deal with continued attacks on his war record by former Confederate officers outraged by his decision to align himself with the Republican Party—none more so than former Confederate general James Lane. Lane's vendetta against Mahone stretched back into the war and was a result of the bloody fight at Spotsylvania's "Mule Shoe" salient on May 12, 1864. Lane's North Carolina brigade captured three enemy flags from Ambrose Burnside's command only to be challenged by Mahone, who claimed that his brigade had secured one of the flags and, further, that the North Carolinians had behaved dishonorably during the fight. A negative portrayal of Lane's performance at Spotsylvania found its way into the De Peyster sketch, which was later revised in the face of Jubal Early's criticisms. Lane also harbored deep resentment against Mahone because of the Virginian's conduct at Reams Station in August 1864, when his men took credit for capturing Union artillery pieces already captured by the North Carolina brigade of Colonel William McRae. Finally, the two sparred over whose men were responsible for the defense of Fort Gregg on April 2, 1865.[30]

Lane enthusiastically joined the growing chorus of attacks against Mahone's leadership of the Readjusters and alliance with congressional Republicans in 1881 by publishing his report on the battle of Spotsylvania, which branded Mahone "a liar and a coward, a man without honor." Even as late as 1890, Lane could not resist an opportunity to challenge Mahone's record. Following the unveiling of the Soldier's Monument at Blandford Cemetery, Lane challenged a number of "false claims" made, including which unit was responsible for the "valuable and heroic defense of Fort Gregg" and the size of the Confederate units surrendered at Appomattox. Lane, venting his frustrations in the pages of the *Southern Historical Society Papers,* was convinced that these "false claims" were "set up . . . at the instance of General Mahone."[31]

Lane's frustration reflected the feelings of betrayal voiced by numerous Confederate veterans and Virginians that continued to reverberate until Mahone's death on October 8, 1895, and beyond. Eulogies proved just how difficult it was for some to distinguish between Mahone's political and military careers. Though the *Norfolk Landmark* applauded Mahone for his "strategic ability," "personal bravery," and "self command," the newspaper concluded that his death "removes one of the most conspicuous figures in the public life of this State since the war." With Mahone's death, Virginia "loses one of her most distinguished sons," suggested the *Portsmouth Star,* and "as an organizer of force, he was unquestionably one of the greatest minds of the age." Still, the *Star* reminded its readers of Mahone's personal legacy: "The name of Virginia was dragged in a mire of reproach and became a by-word and a mockery. From the effects of that political delirium we are just recovering."[32]

The public debate surrounding Mahone's loyalty and military record was not intended simply to get the historical record straight. Mahone's use of his military record to further his own postwar interests provided an easy target for his detractors and serves as a context for understanding what is best described as a reputation war. His leadership of the Readjusters and leadership within the Republican Party threatened such Southern traditions as white supremacy, black subordination, and an agrarian economy with democratic struggle, black political action, and a progressive economic outlook. The legislative agenda of the Readjusters and Mahone's association with the Republicans challenged Lost Cause assumptions that reinforced a conservative political and legislative agenda. That Mahone was not an outsider but rather a successful Confederate major general could not be ignored. Comparing Mahone to John Brown and Benedict Arnold attested to the popular belief that he had betrayed the Southern values fought for in the war. The battles between Mahone and his Lost Cause detractors were not simply about what really happened at the Crater. Instead, they instituted a contest over who could claim legitimate ownership and control of Virginia's Confederate heritage.

Chapter 4

REINFORCING THE STATUS QUO

Reenactment and Jim Crow

CROWDS CHEERED AS the veterans made their way up Second Street on the morning of November 6, 1903. For weeks the City of Petersburg and the A. P. Hill Camp Confederate Veterans had been planning to welcome the veterans to celebrate and reenact the battle of the Crater. The center of attention were the veterans of Major General William Mahone's brigade, who were escorted by veterans' organizations with mounted police and the fire brigade to follow; in the vanguard, serving as chief marshal, was General Stith Bolling. "When the excited thousands saw the veterans made up of every camp," reported a correspondent from the *Richmond Times-Dispatch*, "all bowed, and many lamed, bearing aloft their old battle flag which had been torn literally to shreds by the deadly missiles of the enemy, there arose a cry from ten thousand throats which rent the air and made every heart leap with its contagion." Once on Market Street the members of Mahone's brigade were received by Mahone's widow, who presented each "survivor and each proxy with a handsome badge on which was inscribed the words 'Mahone's Brigade.'"[1]

Finally, the "Crater Legion" arrived at the terminus of the Jerusalem Plank Road and followed the "route by which Mahone's brigade . . . proceeded to the ravine from which the brigade made its charge on that day." Once situated in the ravine, Mahone's veterans listened to an address by Colonel William H. Stewart, who encouraged his men to remember "that we fought for right and justice, for constitutional liberty, for our homes and for our firesides and stand up before all men as proud as a king of the uniform we wore in the Confederate ranks." Around 1:00 p.m., in front of an estimated crowd of 20,000, the veterans charged the area around the crater, now defended by five companies of the Seventieth Regiment and the Richmond Blues, which were given the job of portraying Federal troops. "As soon as Mahone's brigade reached the crest of the hill," reported a correspondent from the *Petersburg Daily Index-Appeal,* "the infantry in the ravine followed firing as rapidly as possible at will as did also the troops in the Crater. The firing of both the artillery and infantry was quick and rapid and the bloodless battle continued for about thirty minutes." After the "sham-battle" the participants were assembled at the Crater, where they were given solid silver medals. The rest of the afternoon was filled with additional speeches and smaller ceremonies, bringing together members of different generations, who listened closely to the personal stories of individual veterans. For the people of Petersburg and the rest of the South, it had been an impressive display of living Confederate history.[2]

By the turn of the century, white Union and Confederate veterans had put aside much of their animosity and claims to the moral high ground, focusing instead on an emotional drive for national unity. While it can be argued that memory of the theme of emancipation and acknowledgment of the crucial role that black soldiers played on the battlefields had been suppressed on the national level, a closer look at Confederate veterans of the Crater suggests a more nuanced story. For veterans of the Crater and other writers, the memory of fighting African American soldiers was never entirely erased, though on more than one occasion—including the 1903 reenactment—organizers of public commemorations of the battle chose to minimize if not omit overt references to this crucial aspect of the battle. In fact, the way Virginia's veterans of the Crater chose to remember this particular experience conformed to changing political conditions and accompanying racial boundaries through Reconstruction, the four years of Readjuster control, and the era of Jim Crow.

Even as the narrative of the battle fostered by the veterans themselves and white Southerners more generally became ever more closely aligned with Virginia's political and racial boundaries at the turn of the twentieth century, black Americans continued to highlight an emancipationist memory of the war that included the heroics of USCTs. Although overshadowed at this time, it would become much more visible during the civil rights movement of the 1950s and 1960s.

In an important sense, the 1903 reenactment functioned as a forum for the meeting of different generations, one representing a lived Confederate history and a younger generation that eagerly embraced the stories

Virginia Military Institute cadets visiting the Crater in June 1915. Mary Custis Lee (in dark clothing) is seated at right, in the front row. (Virginia Military Institute Archives, Lexington)

passed down. Reenactments and reunions provided a unique opportunity not only for veterans to meet with former comrades to discuss shared adventures but, more important, for communities to construct a collective memory of the past based on heroic acts that could then be passed on to their children. Much of that collective memory embraced principles embodied in the Lost Cause, which provided explanations purporting to answer why the Southern states seceded and why the Confederacy lost. These public memories reinforced white social and political superiority backed by Democratic Party solidarity.

The general public was presented with a version of the famous fight at the Crater shaped not only by the veterans' own subjective memory of the experience but also by the Lost Cause tradition and its accompanying political outlook. Evidence for this can be seen in the blatant omission of African American participation in the 1903 reenactment, even though USCTs played an important role at the Crater and were prominently featured in the letters and diaries of Confederates immediately after the battle and in later postwar recollections. There was one "colored man" in the 1903 parade, and his presence reflects an important way in which memory of the Crater had evolved. The individual in question was in fact "Stonewall" Jackson's cook and servant. According to the *Richmond Times-Dispatch,* he "wore the gray of the Confederate soldier, and carried his army canteen. . . ." Frequently he was cheered."[3]

Including Stonewall Jackson's black servant in the procession of veterans leading to the Crater reinforced the goal of submission and compliance to white control. The presence of African Americans at reunions "supported southern racial and political orthodoxies." A rigid social hierarchy with whites at the top could be maintained by encouraging Virginia's black population to honor the "old time negro" who followed his owner into battle to care for him and remained loyal even after the war. By concentrating on black compliance and ignoring memories of bitterness associated with having to fight African Americans at the Crater, elite white Virginians were able to "manage race relations" with a philosophy of paternalism. The 1903 Crater reenactment could not properly depict the role of African Americans in the battle for fear of reminding the local black population of their own steps toward freedom achieved during the Civil War.[4]

The addresses preceding the start of the sham battle, such as the one by William Stewart, made only passing reference to the "brutal malice of negro soldiers." The general themes of the day remained the leadership of William Mahone, whose qualities, according to Robertson Taylor, "were seldom surpassed." The highest praise was reserved for the common soldier: "To the dead as well as to the living, we can render unmeasured praise—to none more than to the private soldier." Stewart's brief reference to the behavior of "negro" soldiers served to remind his audience of black assertiveness during the war and the necessity of maintaining white solidarity without magnifying its importance.[5]

Individual accounts at the turn of the century—many still authored by the veterans themselves—continued to emphasize the belief that black soldiers were coerced into the Union army and were fueled by an irrational rage (or by alcohol) rather than by a conviction that they were engaged in a fight for their freedom. George T. Rogers, who commanded the Sixth Virginia, recalled a conversation with a wounded "colored barber from New York" following the battle. When Rogers inquired "why he did it," the soldier replied "that he was in the army against his will, that he was a drafted man and was obliged to take up his musket, and that, having enlisted, he had done his duty as far as possible." Rogers went on to make the point that a number of captured black soldiers pleaded for their lives: "I ain't fired a shot to-day, Massa. I prays don't kill me." John S. Wise recounted the reaction of those captured black soldiers who before the war had lived in eastern Virginia and who were now face-to-face with their former owners. According to Wise, "the negroes were delighted at the prospect of being treated as slaves, instead of being put to death or sent to a Confederate military prison." The submissiveness and lack of fighting prowess of black soldiers are reflected in another reference to their pleas for mercy. "As they came running into our lines through the dangers of the firing from their own friends," asserted Wise, "they landed among our men, falling on their knees, their eyes rolling in terror, exclaiming, 'Fur God sake, Marster, doan' kill me. Spar' me, Marster, and I'll wuk fur you as long as I lib.'" The frequency of these stories in which soldiers begged for their lives suggests that not a few of these accounts were exaggerated, if not fabricated. Some no doubt included these stories simply as a way to enliven their account, but it might also be the case that veterans and others used them to reinforce their own beliefs of racial superiority throughout the postwar period and in reaction to the changing racial hierarchy—most recently reflected in the Readjuster movement.[6]

The 1903 Crater reenactment in Petersburg marks a significant transition in the way the battle was remembered. What is most striking is the sharp distinction between what individual veterans were willing to share in their accounts of the battle regarding the presence of African American soldiers and the public face of the reenactment itself, which was void of any significant black presence on the battlefield. The tendency on the part of writers to deny black soldiers their manhood by denying their willingness to fight reflected the fear of losing white political control in Virginia at the turn of the century, a fear that was also behind the push toward more stringent segregation laws.

By 1903 Virginians had approved legal segregation practices and disfranchisement as means to prevent a return to the embittered days of Virginia's Readjuster movement, when the state had experimented with black suffrage and interracial political cooperation. In 1900 the General Assembly of Virginia called for a referendum on the holding of a constitutional convention that would overturn the constitution imposed on it during Reconstruction. While the primary goal was to limit the black vote, delegates to the convention substantially reduced the white vote as well with both literacy tests and poll taxes. The new constitution had already succeeded in eliminating the right to vote of all but 21,000 black Virginians of voting age and went on to cut that number in half only three years later. At the same time, and following on the heels of the Supreme Court's decision in *Plessy v. Ferguson* in 1896, the General Assembly in Richmond passed its first Jim Crow law in 1900, which eventually separated the races on streetcars, trains, and in residential neighborhoods. Regulating or "managing" this newly legislated racial hierarchy would take great care on the part of Virginia's white public officials. The public celebration of the Confederate past, including the battle of the Crater, worked to sanction laws that outlined a strict culture of racial segregation and hierarchy.[7]

Though the reenactment and public addresses failed to do justice to the racial components of the battle, the spectrum of emotions associated with having to fight African Americans emerged once again for those who put their memories to paper at this time. Perhaps trying to capitalize on the popularity of the reenactment, William Stewart began collecting recollections from members of his old regiment. Though the accounts are relatively brief, they demonstrate clearly that the aging veterans had little difficulty recalling the horror of battle, the details of close combat, and the number of the enemy they individually killed. Many of the contributors no doubt took part in the reenactment, and this may have made it easier to recall the more visceral emotions that went along with fighting at the Crater, emotions that had been suppressed with time. William Pate, who served in Company D, clearly recalled the cry of "No quarter! Remember Fort Pillow!" and also remembered, "I killed three negroes with the bayonet." At least one Confederate responded to the yelling of "Remember Fort Pillow!" with "Remember Beast Butler." George D. White "commenced firing on the negroes who were trying to get back from the Crater excavation to their lines" and was "certain I killed eight or ten in this manner." William Emerson also remembered "shooting a negro as he ran over the hill trying to escape." Another soldier could not recall how many of the enemy he killed, "and I don't want to know, but I did my best." John T. West of Company A recalled that Confederates were "greatly exasperated" after hearing that blacks were taking part in the battle. "I saw one negro soldier wounded and he was trying to get up off his knees," remembered a soldier in Co. I, "when Laban Godwin hit him in the face with the breech of his gun. . . . I told him to stop that as the negro was dying." Writing a few years later, in 1910, Alfred. L. Scott admitted that "there was considerable stabbing and shooting even after the enemy had thrown down their arms. Some of the officers tried to stop it, while others encouraged it." Though Scott was incensed about the presence of black soldiers, "I was even more so against the whites, as having put arms in their hands and brought them there."[8]

Veterans from outside the Old Dominion also continued to recall with apparent ease the horror of the Crater and their shock, even after forty years, at having to fight black soldiers. W. A. Day, who served in the Forty-ninth North Carolina regiment, shared in very graphic detail the "slaughter" of the Crater. "The soldiers were excited; they were reckless; they burst the negroes' skulls with the butts of their guns like eggshells. The officers tried to prevent it," continued Day, "but they were powerless." A veteran from the Eleventh Alabama regiment described an "odor equaled only by a skunk" as he engaged a black soldier in a brawl within the crater. The scuffle ended only after a comrade "gave the negro a blow on the top of his head that killed him."[9]

The emotionally charged memories of the veterans of the Crater clearly reflect a lingering bitterness at having to fight black soldiers during the war. The individual memories of the veterans contrasted sharply with an evolving public memory that steered clear of overt references to African Americans. These differences in individual and public memories point to competing interests. The strong emotions attached to memories of black soldiers were indelibly stamped in the minds of Confederate veterans. Their inability or unwillingness to ignore or downplay these memories suggests that their own understanding of the significance of this particular battle was closely tied to having to fight black men. On the other hand, public memory of the battle proved to be sufficiently malleable to handle the changing political conditions in postwar Virginia.

The minimizing of the role of black soldiers from Southern accounts of the Crater by the 1880s fit into a broader shift in how Americans chose to remember their Civil War. Few general accounts of the war published before 1900 provided sufficient coverage of black enlistment or of the ways in which their actions on the battlefield altered racial prejudices or contributed to Union victory. In the few cases in which the Crater was mentioned at all, historians chose to minimize or ignore entirely the role of black soldiers. Such a view is reflected clearly in Theodore Ayrault

Dodge's *A Bird's-Eye View of Our Civil War* (1883). In four pages, and in the most general terms, Dodge catalogued the decisions leading to the explosion of the mine and the confusion that defined the Union attack. In all fairness to Dodge, only three names are referenced—Grant, Lee, and Burnside—however, it is difficult to surmise that the absence of black soldiers in his account was integral to the goal of providing the most general account of the war.[10]

The African American veterans of the Fourth Division stood the best chance of being remembered in the pages of newspaper articles and magazine essays authored by their former white officers, who collectively proved to be their greatest advocates. Such postwar accounts reflect both the shared experience of the battlefield and the continuing gulf that existed between the two races. Some white officers wrote about the bravery of USCTs as an extension of their continued work with blacks to uplift the race and promote equal justice. Most simply could not fully account for their own war experience and acts of bravery without referencing their former "colored" comrades.[11]

One of the earliest of these accounts and arguably the most important is Henry G. Thomas's article in *Century Magazine* in 1877. Thomas's article appeared as part of a series of essays on the Civil War that was later republished as the four-volume *Battles and Leaders of the Civil War.* The article guaranteed that a wide popular audience would read about the bravery of the men under his command who, he believed, deserved the "respect of every beholder." Thomas begins his account by conveying the optimism that pervaded the ranks on the eve of their first opportunity to "show the white troops what the colored division could do." The decision to replace the division in the eleventh hour not only leaves the reader wondering what might have happened had the original plan been adhered to, it also absolves the officers and men of responsibility for the disaster.[12]

Writing in 1907 in the pages of the *National Tribune,* Captain D. E. Proctor of the Thirtieth USCT expressed doubt that the veterans of his unit and their descendants would be accepted as full citizens: "It's the white man's burden to settle the question whether a man is a man, without regard to race, color or previous condition. In God's own time it will be settled rightly," Proctor predicted, "but we feel that those who were participants in the great war for the preservation of the Union, and incidentally the freedom of the slave, will never see that day."[13]

For other white officers, the postwar period presented them with a very different burden. The charges of drunkenness leveled at black soldiers at the Crater as well as James Ledlie's record continued to color accounts of the battle as well as the reputations of white officers in the Fourth Division. One officer in the Nineteenth USCT asserted that accusations of drunkenness were "unwarranted by facts." In his own recollection of the battle, published in 1903, J. Q. Adams of the Thirtieth USCT recalled, "I did not see a single officer of colored troops in the slightest degree under the influence." Defending his reputation and those of his fellow white officers, Adams proudly claimed, "The officers of these regiments are the finest body of young men mentally, morally, and physically, that I have ever seen collected together." Adams's vehement defense of soldierly qualities among many white officers reflects a continued belief that the success of the black soldiers could be traced to the moral character and skills of their white officers.[14]

No two former officers of the Fourth Division were more supportive of the black men under their command than Colonel Delavan Bates and Lieutenant Freeman S. Bowley, both from the Thirtieth USCT. Bates authored one of the most extensive accounts of USCTs at the Crater in the pages of the *National Tribune* on January 30, 1908. While Bates did not pass over the opportunity to highlight his own participation in the battle, the brunt of the article focused on the performance of the men in the regiment. More unusual, however, is his commitment to sharing a more personal profile of these men with his readers. Bates recalled a scene on the eve of battle involving the men of Company H, who were gathered to listen to one of their own noncommissioned officers, a preacher before the war.

> My deah bredern, dis am gwine to be er gre't fite de gre'tes' we'uns hab eber seen if we'uns tek Petrsburg mos' likly we'l tuk Richmun, and derstroy Mars Gin'ul Lee's big ahmy and den clos de wah. Ebery man hed orter lif up hiself in praher fur er strong hyart. O, bredern, 'member de pore cullud fokses ober yer in bondage. En 'member Marse Gin'ul Grant, en Marse Gin'ul Burnside, en Marse Gin'ul Meade, en all de uder ob de gre't Gin'uls ober yunner watch'n yer, en, moreover, de fust nigger dat goes ter projeckin' es gwine ter git dis byarnut inter him. 'Fore Gawd, hits sho nuff trufe Ise tellin' yer.

Bates's decision to share in the original dialect what he remembers hearing gives voice to the black veterans of the Crater in a way that they could not do themselves. What emerges is a strong bond built around a shared history of slavery and the hope that their actions on that day would spell its doom. The failure of the attack did nothing to diminish their bravery. According to Bates, "One thing that has been proven, viz, the colored troops dared meet not only in open field the best troops of the Confederacy, but they also dared attack them behind breastworks almost impregnable, and as to results the best standard by which to test the qualities of an army is this: The number killed on the battlefield."[15]

Freeman Bowley authored four accounts of the battle between 1870 and 1899 and, while they differ in detail, he goes to great lengths in each to highlight his own brave conduct on the field as well as that of the men under his command. The nation's failure to acknowledge his men as well as Bowley's own failure to secure a Medal of Honor threatened his sense of honor as a soldier and challenged his conviction that the war had given rise to new freedoms and civil rights to African Americans. Like Bates, Bowley gives voice to the men in his command:

> Of the men of my regiment who had rallied with me all but one, a Sergeant, lay dead or dying. As he stood at my elbow, loading and firing, I said to him, "Sergeant, things are looking very bad for us." . . . "Yes, Lieutenant," he answered, "dey is sho'ly lookin' powerful bad. I reckon, sah, we has to die right yere, sah!" And this was said not in a spirit of bravado, nor in a tone of regret, but as a matter of fact our duty had called us to this place, and it was a part of that duty "to die right yere," and there was no thought of shirking the responsibility.

Bowley's account places him alongside his men in the heat of battle, facing the same dangers and finding a common strength to resist the Confederate tide and possible death.[16]

Even after his capture and imprisonment, Bowley refused to distance himself from the men in his command. Unlike some of his fellow officers, Bowley acknowledged to his captors directly when asked to identify his command: "Thirtieth United States Colored Infantry." Throughout his captivity between Petersburg and Columbia, South Carolina, Bowley withstood the taunts and abuses of white Southerners, who believed that he and the rest of the Union army were "all a miserable lyin' set of thieves, come down yere to steal we'uns niggers." Bowley's memory of these encounters strengthened his own conviction that his service in the USCTs was part of a much larger commitment to emancipation and the betterment of the black race. Although his postwar accounts are sprinkled with stories of reconciliation and reunion, Bowley never backed away from recounting the execution of large numbers of his men after they had surrendered. By 1900 Bowley was one of the few USCT officers who remained committed to challenging a collective memory of the war that had moved away from honoring the service of black soldiers and their role in saving the Union.[17]

The success of the 1903 Crater reenactment functioned to identify the battlefield more closely with the memories of white Virginians as a gallant defense of their homes and their Lost Cause. Throughout this period the African American community in Petersburg and in much of the rest of the nation struggled not only to claim Civil War battlefields such as the Crater as their own but also simply to maintain a presence in the broader collective memory of the war as whites grew increasingly averse to acknowledging the crucial role that USCTs had played in the preservation of the Union as well as in bringing about the end of slavery.

Members of Petersburg's African American community may have been in a much stronger position, relative to other communities, to publicly celebrate and commemorate their participation in the late war. The city had a sizeable free black population even as late as 1860, which remained active in the community. During the 1870s and 1880s, the black population was even in number with the white population. Blacks enjoyed the benefits of citizenship, including educational opportunities, expanded civil rights, a voice in the courts, enfranchisement, and political office-holding. It was due to the success of the Readjuster movement that Petersburg's black population continued to enjoy those benefits at a time when other states succumbed to "Redeemer" governments after the official end of Reconstruction in 1877.[18]

Deeply rooted institutions such as the church as well as a broad range of fraternal organizations supported political, economic, and social activities within the black community. The community stayed informed of the many happenings in the area through a growing number of newspapers, including (at different times) the *Petersburg Lancet, Afro-American Churchman, American Sentinel, National Pilot,* and *Herald.* Such a vibrant community and active press made it possible to promote and commemorate significant moments in recent black history as well as to remain connected with commemorative movements outside of Virginia. The efforts of African Americans in Petersburg and elsewhere to celebrate their past was intended to show that they had contributed all along to the growth of the nation and that they had earned their rights as citizens through their willingness to make the same sacrifices as white Americans during the war.[19]

The creation of several black militia companies proved to be one of the most successful ways to instill civic spirit in the community as well as to provide a vehicle for the remembrance of black military service. The Petersburg Guards were organized in June 1873, followed by the Flipper Guards in 1877 and, finally, the Petersburg Blues in 1878. The three Petersburg militias joined companies from places such as Richmond, Staunton, Danville, and Fredericksburg and at their height in 1880 numbered approximately 1,000 members. The companies primarily served a social and recreational function, including participation in local and state ceremonies and four presidential inaugurations. In Petersburg the companies could be seen leading the parades that marked Lincoln's Emancipation Proclamation on January 1 and Independence Day on July 4. On July 4, 1875, white militia joined the Petersburg Guards for the largest Independence Day celebration since the Civil War.[20]

Local appearances and public drills offered ample opportunity to commemorate the heroism of the region's black veterans. On the occasion of the tenth anniversary of the formation of the Petersburg Guards, A. W. Harris, a local black member of the General Assembly, addressed the company, calling on them to remember the bravery of black soldiers during the Haitian revolt of 1802 as well as their role in such Civil War battles as Fort Wagner and Olustee. That same year, another local politician, George Fayerman, implored the militia and the rest of Petersburg's African American community to reject the commonly held belief that they had no military tradition. Referencing the likes of Toussaint L'Overture and the Carthaginian general Hannibal, Fayerman said, "It makes my blood boil to hear people say that the colored man cannot fight." It is unknown why the Crater fight was not mentioned in either speech, but the fact that a slave revolt and its leader were openly celebrated in Petersburg in 1883 attests to the continued black influence in local and state politics.[21]

However effective commemorative speeches proved to be in forging a collective memory within the black community of Petersburg, they could not compete with the growing trend among white Virginians to dedicate monuments in public spaces that reflected their own selective memory of the war. The period between 1870 and 1910 witnessed the erection of impressive monuments such as the Lee statue on Monument Avenue in Richmond in 1890 as well as countless generic soldier monuments gracing the lawns of just about every county courthouse in Virginia. If the African American community were to participate in this process, it would have to find a way both to influence the local political apparatus and to raise the necessary funds—both of which proved difficult during this time. The *Petersburg Lancet* urged its readers to "never cease to praise the valor of their sacred dead, and to create monuments in their honor. O! ingratitude and shame on the colored people of the United States, who show such little appreciation for the valor of negro soldiers who died for the preservation of the Union." Perhaps remembering the failed assault at the Crater, the editorial exhorted its readers to support "a monument to the black heroes, who leaped over the fortification [at Petersburg] with their muskets in our defense and suffered their bodies as it were to become breastworks while pouring out their blood most freely and willingly for our redemption from bondage." Black activists made numerous attempts to add the black soldier to the commemorative landscape across the South, but by the end of the nineteenth century only three monuments depicted blacks in military service—and they were all located in the North.[22]

The loss of political leverage following the defeat of the Readjusters, along with the challenge of raising the necessary financial resources, left the black community in Petersburg with little hope of being able to add to the region's growing number of Civil War monuments or shape other public spaces. By the early twentieth century, political disfranchisement, along with a short and ultimately unsuccessful deployment during the Spanish-American War that was plagued by problems with the unit's white commander, led to the end of the black militias. Even though the governor called out the black militia only once during its existence, it effectively functioned as the one place where members of the black community in Petersburg could publicly commemorate and nurture a collective past that connected them to the Civil War through the men who had fought in it.[23]

If the rise of Jim Crow represented the nadir of the black community's ability to celebrate its collective past in public, it did not extinguish it completely. Rather, black leaders emphasized their shared heritage by continuing the fight for civil and political rights as well as for improvements in education and the economic condition of the race. The segregation of public schools did have the positive effect of creating a space where African Americans could develop a black historical consciousness outside of the purview of whites and in opposition to their preferred historical view. That isolation, however, came with the price of being pushed further away from public institutions that whites used to disseminate their history, which in turn worked to reinforce their control of local, state, and national government.[24]

Not surprisingly, few accounts of African American participation in the war were published during this time. The few that did surface received favorable reviews—most notably George W. Williams's *History of the Negro Race in America from 1619–1880* (1883) and *A History of the Negro Troops in the War of the Rebellion* (1888). At the age of fourteen, Williams enlisted in the Union in 1863, later enlisting in the Mexican army to aid in the government's fight against French colonists. Upon returning to the United States, in 1867 Williams enlisted again in the U.S. Army, serving for one year on the frontier. Williams later served as pastor of the Twelfth Street Baptist Church in Boston and in 1879 he became the first African American to serve in the Ohio legislature.

Williams led the way in presenting African American history accurately through the use of oral history and archival research, seeking to legitimize it as a field of historical study. In an attempt to encourage the preservation of a black historical consciousness, Williams joined others in calling for the creation of an American Negro Historical Society. His *History of the Negro Troops* offers a detailed account of the experiences and challenges USCTs faced during the Civil War, and access to the newly published *Official Records* made it possible for Williams to provide ample coverage of their performance on the various battlefields. At times, however, it is difficult not to read into this study a sense of Williams's desperation concerning the difficulty of conveying the full significance of the sacrifice made by black men to his readers:

> The part enacted by the Negro in the war of the Rebellion is the romance of North American history. It was midnight and noonday without a space between; from the Egyptian darkness of bondage to the lurid glare of civil war; from clanking chains to clashing arms; from passive submission to the cruel curse of slavery to the brilliant aggressiveness of a free soldier; from a chattel to a person; from the shame of degradation to the glory of military exaltation; and from

deep obscurity to fame and martial immortality. No one in this era of fraternity and Christian civilization will grudge the Negro soldier these simple annals of his trials and triumphs in a holy struggle for human liberty. Whatever praise is bestowed upon his noble acts will be sincerely appreciated, whether from former foes or comrades in arms. For by withholding just praise they are not enriched, nor by giving are they thereby impoverished.

Although Williams's broad moral observation about the meaning of black military service is easily interpreted as a response to the growing call for reunion between white Americans, it must also be understood as a reflection of racial pride that he hoped blacks would continue to embrace even as the fruits of that sacrifice were being stripped away.[25]

Williams's desire to account for the bravery of the USCTs at the Crater led to a few literary flourishes, such as the claim that "three veteran white divisions had been hurled back in confusion" before the Fourth Division had been ordered to advance. And one wonders if Williams would have confidently asserted, "The Negro soldier's valor was, after this engagement, no more questioned than his loyalty" if he had had access to the accounts written by the black troops' white comrades in the wake of the battle. Given the amount of attention Williams devoted to the battle and his apparent commitment to doing justice to the service of black soldiers, it may seem strange that he does not reference the slaughter of captured soldiers. His acknowledgment and detailed overview of Fort Pillow adds to the mystery, but it should be remembered that the volume of the *Official Records* that covers the Crater was not published until 1892. In other words, Williams may not have known that there was a large-scale massacre or, if he did, he may not have been able to accurately judge its scope.[26]

Edward A. Johnson, principal of the Washington School in Raleigh, North Carolina, chose to include a detailed discussion of the Crater in his history of African Americans to provide his students with "information on the many brave deeds and noble characters of their own race." Johnson was all too aware of the lack of attention given to African Americans: "The Negro is hardly given a passing notice in many of the histories taught in the schools; he is credited with no heritage of valor; he is mentioned only as a slave, while true historical records prove him to have been among the most patriotic of patriots, among the bravest of soldiers, and constantly a God-fearing, faithful producer of the nation's wealth." In Johnson's history of the Crater his students could read about Ambrose Burnside's decision to place his black soldiers at the head of the attacking column (or "post of honor") and the final decision to replace them with a white division, which ultimately led to disaster. Johnson described this decision as a "ridiculous mistake," citing the testimony of Grant, who argued that if Burnside had relied on his original plan, the attack "would have been a success." "Four Thousand Four Hundred Union soldiers perished," according to Johnson, "through the mistake then of not allowing the colored troops to take the Confederate works." As for the conduct of the black soldiers on the battlefield, Johnson praised their bravery and even included Confederate references to the screams of "No quarter!" which was reinterpreted as evidence that they would have their work cut out for them in securing the salient.[27]

Others works of merit were published at this time, including Joseph T. Wilson's *The Black Phalanx* (1890), which offers extensive coverage of the history of black military service going back to the American Revolution. As much as these accounts by black historians offered a much-needed corrective to the prevailing view, many are written in a "defensive" style, as their authors were forced to respond to critics who relied on stereotypes and the newly emerging "scientific" evidence of racial inferiority. The need to defend their "manly honor" on the battlefield was only compounded by the humiliation caused by the gradual winnowing away of their civil liberties.[28]

By the beginning of the twentieth century, white Virginians had succeeded in stamping the Crater battlefield, as well as the war as a whole, with their preferred memory. That memory highlighted the battle as a gallant defense of home and lauded the performance of the Virginia brigade and Mahone's leadership as responsible for Confederate victory that day. The fact of USCTs' participation at the Crater was either ignored entirely or carefully controlled so as not to remind the community that black men had attempted to secure their own freedom. This served to unite white Virginians around a shared set of values that bound them together with their Confederate ancestors and functioned to justify a return to a political system that excluded blacks. For the veterans of the battle, however, time did not diminish the impact of having to engage black men in close combat. They recalled the spectrum of emotions that gave meaning to their experiences that day and, on occasion, recorded their memories for their community and posterity.

The triumph of reunion and reconciliation in the country's collective memory of the Civil War pushed memory of the role of African American soldiers and the theme of emancipation from the national stage. The tendency for public commemorations of the Crater (along with other commemorative events at the turn of the century) to ignore the participation of black soldiers and the racially infused memories of the battle's veterans all but guaranteed that USCTs at the Crater would be erased from the historical landscape until the civil rights movement in the 1960s. The setbacks associated with segregation and Jim Crow, however, did not prevent African Americans from taking steps to commemorate and preserve a historical record of their role in the war and the contributions of black soldiers to saving the Union.

Chapter 5

WHITES ONLY

The Ascendancy of an Interpretation

THE "SUCCESS" OF the 1903 reunion and reenactment—as well as plans to hold the event on a yearly basis—renewed interest in creating a national park in Petersburg with the Crater as one of the principal sites. Support came not only from the city of Petersburg and the rest of Virginia but also from states north of the Potomac River. The outbreak of war with Spain in 1898 fostered deeper sectional reconciliation and gave Southerners "an opportunity to free themselves of Northern suspicion of their loyalty and to establish southern honor." Ex-Confederate generals such as Fitzhugh Lee, who had served two years as consul in Havana, and Joseph Wheeler embraced the war and received wide acclaim; both were commissioned as major generals of volunteers. Closer to home, increased contact between Union and Confederate veterans in Petersburg forged personal bonds that carried over into the push to create a national park.[1]

Early interest in establishing a park in Petersburg formed part of a larger national phenomenon that included the opening of Shiloh, Chickamauga, Chattanooga, Antietam, Gettysburg, and Vicksburg National Military Parks—all in the 1890s. Beginning in the 1880s, increased interaction between veterans on both sides promoted feelings of patriotism, nationalism, and reconciliation as the Civil War soldier became the primary focus of attention, while the themes of slavery, emancipation, and the service of African American soldiers faded.

In contrast to other cities founding military parks, Petersburg struggled to find the right balance between preserving its Confederate past and expanding its commercial economy in the present. Although Confederate veterans might embrace their onetime enemies on old battlefields such as the Crater, they remained cautious about plans to develop these sites originating from outside Virginia. More important, while sectional reconciliation and reunion constituted an important backdrop to the efforts of various actors—Northern and Southern—to preserve Petersburg's Civil War battlefields, local heritage preservationists remained committed to maintaining a narrative of the battle that reflected a faithfulness to Virginia's Lost Cause. The future of the Crater site specifically remained uncertain throughout this time and reflected the uneasy mix of heritage preservation and commercial development. As a result, Petersburg did not establish a National Military Park that included the Crater until 1936.

One of the earliest examples of reconciliation involving the Crater took place just a few months after the end of the war. Writing from Alexandria, Virginia, in June 1865, Captain Fred E. Waldron of the Fifty-first New York Volunteers contacted Ella Merrit in South Carolina to inform her that the grave of her relative had been located on the Crater battlefield. Captain Waldron first noticed the grave following the final push to capture Confederate "works in front of Petersburg" at the beginning of April. The soldier had served in the Seventeenth South Carolina and, as indicated by the date on the marker, was killed during the battle. There is some evidence that Waldron was already on friendly terms with the Merrits, though the nature and extent of their relationship is unclear. Perhaps assuming that the Merrit family had insufficient funds for reburial, Waldron indicated that Ella Merrit need "not feel under any obligations to me for it would afford me a great pleasure to do any of your family a favor that is in my power." Union veterans traveling to the site of the battle made other attempts at reconciliation in the following decades.[2]

Almost two decades later, in October 1883, a group of Union veterans from a Grand Army of the Republic (GAR) post in Newark, New Jersey, toured the Crater battlefield during a visit to Petersburg. Two years later, about thirty members of the Fifty-first Pennsylvania Regiment traveled to Petersburg. Before touring the battlefields, they were welcomed by Mayor Jarratt and other dignitaries at the depot and escorted to a hotel. The members of the group toured the area around Fort Stedman searching for relics, and while at the Crater they held their annual business meeting, at which new officers were elected, and passed a resolution thanking the City of Petersburg for its "kind reception and hospitality." Later that evening the veterans were welcomed at the residence of William Mahone for a glass of champagne and an "hour's conversation in the most pleasant way, discussing the Crater fight."[3]

The Crater was a popular site for reunions of Confederates as well as Union veterans. Increased interaction between former enemies encouraged the preservation of the site. The Fifty-seventh Massachusetts Regiment traveled to Petersburg in 1887. William Mahone stands at the center of the first row (with white beard). (Virginia Historical Society, Richmond)

During the first week of May 1887, a larger group of veterans, from the Fifty-seventh and Fifty-ninth Massachusetts regiments, traveled to Petersburg. Like their predecessors from Pennsylvania, the veterans toured Fort Stedman and the Crater, where they listened to speeches by one of the regiment's officers and by William Mahone. Lieutenant C. H. Pinkham's address at Fort Stedman recalled the unit's role in the battle and encouraged his listeners to "remember the brave lives that were sacrificed on that early March morning." In his address at the Crater, Mahone downplayed the fighting prowess of his men and the horrific scenes witnessed; instead he emphasized his concern at the time that the Union attack was likely to succeed, "for we could not have got away." "We could not have got off a piece of artillery," Mahone continued, "and the infantry could only have scampered back. I reckoned we were gone up." Later that afternoon, the veterans returned to their hotel for a meeting to elect officers. The trip ended with a visit to Mahone's residence, where they were "hospitably entertained." In this conciliatory spirit, Mahone's speech, like others, tended to minimize the Northern defeat for the purpose of strengthening ties with his guests around shared values—and neither side risked mentioning the presence of USCTs.[4]

Early visits by Union veterans led to the first concerted effort to purchase the site for preservation. In early March 1896 the *New York Times* reported that a syndicate of GAR units was interested in purchasing the site for the construction of a soldiers' home and to ensure that the battlefield would be open to future commemorative ceremonies. Those involved ultimately hoped to turn the Crater into a "beautiful National park" and thus bring into "prominence one of the finest sites in Virginia." It is unknown why these plans never materialized; however, it should be remembered that the 1903 reenactment had been orchestrated specifically to highlight the bravery of Virginians at a time during the war when decisive victories were rare. It is likely that local officials and the veterans themselves were skeptical about the idea of a sacred piece of Southern land being placed under the auspices of a predominantly Northern organization. Ultimately, the resistance to such an idea points to the limits of reunion and reconciliation.[5]

Reunions between former enemies continued into the first decade of the twentieth century. In 1907 a large contingent of Pennsylvanians representing the Forty-eighth Pennsylvania, including the governor, traveled to Petersburg, where they were greeted by Virginia's governor, Claude A. Swanson, and the A. P. Hill Camp Confederate Veterans. The veterans traveled together on the city's new electric streetcars to the Crater, where they unveiled a new monument to the men who constructed the mineshaft and listened to addresses by the two governors. The address by William J. Wells, who had served with the unit, concentrated on common values, shared history, and the conviction that the men on both sides did what they "believed to be right." Wells echoed the new feelings of nationalism, noting, "We who fought here are enabled without the loss of manly dignity, to grasp each other's hand in national pride, and to recall the events of 1861–65, in which we took so conspicuous a part, only to laud each the deeds of the other."[6]

Two years later, veterans from the Third Division of the Ninth Corps made their way to Petersburg to dedicate a monument. In a spirit of friendship, the A. P. Hill Camp and the wife of William Mahone assisted with the unveiling of the monument. The invocation included a plea that "all feelings of sectional strife be entirely forgotten and blotted out." By dedicating monuments on the Crater battlefield and other places around Petersburg, Northern veterans identified with the need to set aside land to be protected as a national park. The emphasis in both sides' speeches on the bravery of the common soldier allowed the veterans to concentrate on shared values rather than on the divisive topic of emancipation and the lingering bitterness among Confederate veterans concerning the presence of black soldiers. The content of these speeches also worked to unite the veterans in the shared goal of saving battlefields regardless of their location.[7]

Public awareness was growing that major Civil War sites were disappearing and that attention to preservation would highlight the importance of the Crater. One visitor to the battlefield reported that "the only thing remaining to-day of the massive lines of earthworks which encircled Petersburg and extended for more than twenty miles, is the 'crater,' which is an object of great interest to visitors on account of the novel part it played in the war of the rebellion." The deterioration in and around the Crater battlefield was apparent to another visitor in 1916. "The land companies and farmers have already demolished a number of old forts and war landmarks," commented John S. Wood of Norfolk, Virginia, "and in a few years the crater itself, in which so many thousands of lives were lost, will be leveled off in all probability." Wood took advantage of sectional reconciliation to draw attention to the sacrifice made by both sides at the Crater. "In the crater are growing pine trees and elms enriched by the blood of 5,000 soldiers of both sides. The crater is still a deep hollow, a sacred valley of death."[8]

The push in the Old Dominion to set aside land in Petersburg and other parts of Virginia lagged behind such activity in other states. Battlefields were seen as sites where visitors could exercise their imaginations, "bring back the contending armies; the roar of cannon; the rattle of musketry; the smoke-pall; the charges of armed men; the shouts of victory, and the stern silence of defeat." Writing for the *Metropolitan* magazine, John D. Wells worried that Virginia's battlefields "may alter greatly," to the point where the imagination would be unable to conjure up the "conditions on the day of the struggle." By the time of the publication of this article in 1907, steps had already been taken on both the local and state level to guarantee that sections of Virginia's landscape would remain unharmed, including the placement of monuments and other markers; however, without oversight by the state and/or the federal government, Petersburg's battlefields remained open to development and ruin.[9]

While the rhetoric behind the preservation of the Crater and other Petersburg battlefields highlighted themes of national reunion and the Confederacy's Lost Cause, concerns regarding the city's economic difficulties complicated the situation. Beginning in 1900, census figures reflect a decline in population, which continued into the 1930s. There are a number of reasons for this, including the obstruction of the Appomattox River into Petersburg, which hindered trade, and the closing of the city's cotton and tobacco factories—though the tobacco factories did return beginning in the 1950s. In addition, the city experienced the gradual disappearance of its commission merchants as their merchandising methods became obsolete.[10]

Captain Carter R. Bishop of the A. P. Hill Camp Confederate Veterans and cashier of the Appomattox Trust Company understood the economic benefits battlefield preservation would yield for the Petersburg area. In 1907 Bishop published a pamphlet for the Petersburg City Council that highlighted the possibilities of promoting local tourism as a way to improve the economy. With the success of the 1903 reenactment fresh in mind, Bishop sought to attract tourists from all over the country by citing the heroic acts of the veterans on both sides. Petersburg was a place where "Grant met Lincoln for the last time" as well as where "Davis and Lee held a council of war." More specifically, Bishop hoped to attract federal funds for the construction of a new military base. In doing so, he connected the practical benefits of locating the base in Petersburg with the necessity of preserving the area's battlefields: "If the military students of Europe think it worth while to come here to collect material for the text-books, is it not true wisdom on the part of the country to hand down intact to her soldiers . . . the most impressive volume on the Art of War?" Although Bishop's work eventually paid off with the completion of Fort Lee in 1917, the question of how to preserve the battlefields and under whose authority remained.[11]

Fort Lee was located in close proximity to the Crater and other significant sites from the siege. Its completion highlights the problem that Petersburg faced in the early twentieth century as it struggled to balance ways to improve the local economy and preserve important historical sites. Veterans' reunions and reenactments stamped the Crater landscape with profound meaning for significant cross sections of the local population, the rest of Virginia, and beyond, but it was still in doubt whether the site would succumb to the pressures of a struggling economy.[12]

Between 1898 and 1906, a series of bills in the House of Representatives and proposals in Virginia state government to create a park failed to generate sufficient support. Multiple proposals to create commissions to survey land and generate plans, ranging from the building of a memorial road from Gettysburg to Petersburg to a memorial road planned for Petersburg, came and went. In 1907 residents of Petersburg continued to push national and state legislators to introduce resolutions for the creation of a park. Newspapers reminded their readers that although a park would benefit the entire country, local residents needed "to take the initiative in such an undertaking and it is clearly in their interest and their duty to do so." In contributing to the call for a national park, Virginian congressman Walter A. Watson concluded that "the site of the explosion is still the most interesting spot . . . made famous by the War between the States, and the Crater is annually visited by thousands of tourists from all parts of the country":

> Three states of the North, Maine, Pennsylvania and Massachusetts, have erected monuments already to their dead on the battlefields around Petersburg, and other States would very gladly do so but for the obstacles they encounter in having to buy sites from the owners of private property. If the government purchased sufficient ground near Petersburg, and dedicated it to the use of the veterans of both armies as a national park, this difficulty would be overcome, and monuments to the memory of soldiers of the various commands, North and South, would spring up as if by magic. The value of these to the present generation, to posterity and to the truth of history would be more than commensurate with the cost to the government, to say nothing of the encouragement to patriotism of the inspiring example of a government that gratefully testifies to the memory of the men who died in its behalf. A people who forget their dead deserve themselves to be forgotten.

Watson's supporters understood that the purchase of various battlefield sites would further sectional reconciliation and would allow for the continued dedication of monuments, which would work toward satisfying future generations' interest in the Civil War.[13]

In April 1907, Charles Hall Davis, the well-known Petersburg lawyer and chairman of the Chamber of Commerce Battlefield Park Committee, proposed a reenactment of the battle of the Crater with the support of the A. P. Hill Camp. With the success of the 1903 reenactment still fresh in mind, Davis hoped to galvanize public support and finally establish a battlefield park by highlighting both the benefits to Petersburg's economy and heritage preservation. The *Daily Index-Appeal* thought it an opportune moment, since "the eyes of the whole country" would be directed toward Virginia for the scheduled Jamestown Exposition. The Petersburg City Council was asked to appropriate $5,000 for the event, but owing to legal restrictions was unable to do so. Though disappointed, Davis suggested that the Crater farm—still owned by the Griffith family—might be purchased as a first step in the creation of a national battlefield park. The failure to gain the support of the city council had not stopped the plans for the 1903 reenactment. However, the goal of staging a much more elaborate event proved to be too difficult, and on May 19, 1907, readers of Petersburg's newspapers learned that the "sham battle at the Crater" had been cancelled.[14]

Despite the failure to stage the reenactment, Northerners continued to express interest in helping the residents of Petersburg with their plans to establish a park. Proposals for the park attracted the attention of James Anderson of Springfield, Massachusetts, a Union veteran who had fought at Petersburg. Known as "Colonel Jim," he was an honorary member of the A. P. Hill Camp, and every year since 1896 had traveled to Virginia to observe R. E. Lee's birthday with Confederate veterans. Although his father had sympathized with the South, Anderson had run away at the age of fifteen to enlist as a private in the Thirty-first Maine Infantry, which served in General Robert Potter's division. In the local papers Anderson proposed that the A. P. Hill Camp send a delegation to a Northern GAR camp to enlist its support. In late 1907 Senator Nathan B. Scott of West Virginia, who had served in the Eighty-eighth Regiment Ohio Volunteer Infantry, introduced a joint resolution that called for an examination of the Petersburg battlefields to determine the advisability of establishing a park; his effort proved to be no more successful than previous endeavors. Virginia congressman Frank R. Lassiter continued the work by proposing a resolution to survey the battlefields around Petersburg. This resolution eventually ended up in the hands of the War Department, where General

William W. Wotherspoon, assistant chief of staff, agreed to assign his department the task of conducting the Petersburg battlefield surveys.[15]

At the same time Lassiter was advocating for the necessary surveys of
land, in 1909 a plan to construct a "Gettysburg to Petersburg Memorial
Road" was proposed by Charles H. Davis. Davis's plan was not without
critics. Lassiter informed him that the Committee on Military Affairs was
skeptical, and that such a plan would be more difficult to pass than legislation for a park. The plan won the support of New York native Colonel
Archibald Gracie, who was known to have some influence in Washington's diplomatic and legislative circles and whose father, Brigadier General
Archibald Gracie Jr., had been killed at Petersburg in December 1864.
Gracie pushed to create an association to steer the proposal through the
necessary channels and worked tirelessly transmitting petitions for a park
to veterans' organizations and others. His efforts and political connections
were not enough, however, and yet another plan died.

Local organizations, newspapers, and the City of Petersburg continued to push for the park. It is difficult to explain the barriers that individuals and organizations on the local and national level faced in creating
a national park. The lack of any strict boundary between preserved earthworks and a growing area of commercial development around Petersburg
in the decades since the war no doubt made it difficult to envision a large
area of land set aside for the general public. Battlefield parks at Gettysburg, Shiloh, and Chickamauga were either isolated from commercial
development or situated in a way that made them easier to survey and
organize. The nature of the fighting around Petersburg may also have
delayed recognition of the need to involve the federal government in preservation. The ten-month siege of Petersburg was defined by the day-to-day
grind of life in earthworks rather than by the elaborate movements of
troops or sophisticated flanking maneuvers that could be followed by
visitors at other sites. Finally, although the Crater was the most popular
tourist destination in the Petersburg area, until 1918 it was open to visitors
only because the Griffith family saw economic benefits in maintaining
the battlefield.

Even without much success on the legislative front, the continued interaction between Union and Confederate veterans and the interest of the
general public highlighted the importance of government oversight. In the
days following the dedication of a monument at the Crater by the Com-

The economic development of Petersburg at the turn of the
twentieth century spurred interest in bringing the Crater site
under public control. (Petersburg National Battlefield)

monwealth of Massachusetts in November 1911, local newspapers were
quick to acknowledge the close connection and support from the North.
"As each monument is placed the interest of the state erecting it becomes
permanent," asserted the editor of the *Petersburg Daily Index-Appeal*, "and
the representatives of these states will undoubtedly favor the entire tract of
land being acquired by the government for park purposes." And in the end
this would guarantee "national supervision and caretaking." The A. P.

Hill Camp worked to publicize visits by Northern veterans to focus national attention on the battlefields of Petersburg. An elaborate banquet for the veterans of Massachusetts, along with the governor, provided an opportunity to toast their mutual interest in preserving what had become sacred ground for the entire nation.[16]

Not until 1923 was there to be another concerted effort to establish a national park, this time under the leadership of Carter R. Bishop. Bishop worked closely with Congressman Patrick H. Drewry and other notable public figures, such as James Anderson of Massachusetts, who convinced the Speaker of the House of Representatives to introduce legislation in Congress. The bill once again went through the War Department and then to the Committee of Military Affairs for review, though the secretary of war was not a supporter of adding additional battlefield parks. Bishop quickly obtained the support of influential Northern politicians such as the governor of Pennsylvania and Senator James W. Wadsworth. Congressman Drewry's bill, which was submitted on April 29, 1924, was finally passed on February 11, 1925. The bill provided for the creation of a commission appointed by the secretary of war to study the feasibility of organizing the battlefield sites for the purposes of tourism and military study. The day that so many had waited for finally arrived on July 3, 1926, when President Calvin Coolidge signed the bill authorizing the establishment of the Petersburg National Military Park. The United Daughters of the Confederacy, the Sons of Confederate Veterans, individual veterans, and Northern states were singled out for praise by the *New York Times*: "The effort to establish a battlefield park here has a history marked by enduring perseverance."[17]

The Petersburg Battlefield Park Association was created to raise money to acquire land and then transfer it to the federal government. Residents of Petersburg responded to the financial needs of the park by raising funds for surveying and for descriptive plates to guide visitors. One such meeting held in October 1926 raised over $1,400; the principal speaker was Douglas S. Freeman, whose growing scholarly reputation placed him at the forefront of Civil War historians. Freeman had had a close connection with Petersburg and specifically with the Crater since his attendance at the 1903 reenactment with his father, Walker H. Freeman, who had served in the Thirty-fourth Virginia. The seventeen-year-old Freeman was moved by the events of the day; he had been raised on his father's stories about the war and had absorbed the tenets of the Lost

Cadets took part in the dedication of the Petersburg National Military Park on June 20, 1932. The Crater site would not be included in the park for another five years. (Petersburg Museums)

Cause. On this day, however, Freeman was inspired to action as the result of what he saw. "If someone doesn't write the story of these men," Freeman wrote in his diary, "it will be lost forever." Rather than see that story lost to posterity, he resolved to himself, "I'm going to do it." The 1903 reenactment of the Crater propelled Douglas Southall Freeman down the road toward completing two major historical projects, one a four-volume Pulitzer Prize–winning biography of Lee, and the other a three-volume study of Lee's lieutenants.[18]

The perseverance of park supporters was finally rewarded on the morning of June 20, 1932, as formal dedication ceremonies for the Petersburg National Military Park took place at Battery Five. Several thousand attended, and a full holiday was declared for Petersburg's summer school sessions so that students could attend the ceremony and afternoon pageant. Though the ceremony included local dignitaries and representatives from Confederate veterans groups, the inclusion of representatives from the North reminded everyone that creation of the military park was a product of national cooperation. Virginia congressman Patrick H. Drewry pointed out that the park was the result not only of the efforts of the people of Petersburg, Virginians, and Southerners, but that "no greater help was rendered in the matter than by the citizens of the State of Massachusetts, for whose help we here express our gratitude." The dedicatory address by the assistant secretary of war, Frederick H. Payne of Massachusetts, reflected the feelings of shared accomplishment and anticipated the continued value of a national park for all Americans: "The opportunity has been provided for Americans of all time to draw inspiration from the valor, the patriotism, the devotion and the loyalty of the men who wore the Blue and of those who wore the Gray."[19]

Though the creation of the national park was a milestone, it would not include the Crater until 1936. Throughout the first half of the 1920s, attendance at the Crater remained steady. "There are signs everywhere urging all to visit that tragic site," recalled one visitor. "Today the crater road is well laid, and one Sunday this Summer as many as eighty-two visitors rode over it after 3 o'clock in the afternoon." The failure to include the most popular Civil War battlefield in Petersburg in the new park reflected the continued tension between heritage preservation and commercial development.[20]

In 1918 the Crater site passed from the Griffith family, and in 1925 it was acquired by the Crater Battlefield Association, Inc., a commercial enterprise that erected a clubhouse near the crater and an eighteen-hole golf course. The association continued to maintain the small building housing a museum, allowing visitors to tour what remained of the mine for a small fee. It is difficult to imagine golfers not being constantly reminded that their course was at one point a terrible bloodletting or that the largest sand trap once contained the mangled bodies of young men. "The golf links extend up to the site of the old fort," reported one visitor, and on an adjacent ridge "a visitor to the battlefield may observe the storms and changes of more than sixty years."[21]

Owners of the golf course attempted to assuage the concerns of preservationists by maintaining a path to what remained of the actual crater. The association provided visitors with a short brochure describing the battle written by its president, Arthur W. James. His account highlighted themes that had become standard in histories of the battle, including the role Mahone and his Virginia brigade played in saving Lee's army; not surprisingly, the presence of African American soldiers was minimized. The last few paragraphs were reserved to promote relations between the corporation and the surrounding community, which may have been strained, considering the popular belief that the Crater should have been incorporated into the National Park. James described his "corporation as composed of Virginia people interested in its preservation and restoration. . . . As a labor of love and at large personal expense, the members of the corporation cleared the battlefield opened the Pleasants galleries, finding the greater part intact, built a road to the site, and opened the sacred spot to visitors." The president hoped to convince visitors that the golf course was an appropriate addition to the battlefield and the result of cooperation with local, state, and national organizations. James closed with what he probably assumed to be a moving tribute to those who had made the ultimate sacrifice on July 30, 1864: "The Crater, covered by giant pines and cedars, immortalizing the soldiers with whose bodies they have been enriched, perfumed with honeysuckle now spread over the reddened trenches, marked by numerous monuments placed by comrades and descendents, surrounded by green fairways and tees bearing the name of its heroes, is a beautiful shrine to the boys of the Blue and Gray who there made the supreme sacrifice."[22]

It is difficult to imagine that James's defense of his company's good intentions persuaded interested parties that their preservation worries were misplaced. In the end, the failure to incorporate the Crater site into the new park suggests the influence that commercial interests held at a time when Petersburg's economy continued to suffer. Neither the efforts of prominent local and national public officials nor those of the veterans themselves were enough to transfer ownership from private to public hands.[23]

Only after the association and the Crater Golf Club closed was the federal government able to purchase the site in 1936. Most of the summer and fall of 1937 was spent removing golf traps and greens; trees and shrubs were planted to shield the field from modern structures along nearby highways. A restoration of the entrance to the mineshaft was also started in 1937. Workers uncovered shell fragments, nails, and other articles as the work progressed. Excavations indicated that the starting point of the tunnel corresponded with the location of the stone monument placed there by the veterans of the Forty-eighth Pennsylvania in 1907. In November 1937, the remains of two Union soldiers were found.[24]

In addition to physical improvements to the landscape, park officials erected markers outlining the battle. The content of these markers reflected an interpretation that by the turn of the century had become standard. The overall mission of the Petersburg National Military Park was to "commemorate the valor and devotion of the American soldiers of the Revolution and the War Between the States." Visitors were expected to interpret the battlefield as a site "on which the manhood of the North and of the South, each contending for high ideals, engaged in the final decisive struggles of the war of 1861–1865." Such an interpretation left no room to acknowledge the battle as a moment for African American soldiers to demonstrate their willingness to sacrifice their lives for freedom because they played no role in the development of the public memory of the battle. There was no mention of the rage exhibited by Confederates at having to fight black soldiers or of the well-documented incidents involving their execution after they surrendered. George Bernard's *War Talks of Confederate Veterans* was used as a reference to describe the Confederate counterattack. As a result, Mahone's Virginia brigade was singled out as the most important component leading to Confederate success: one marker, titled "Mahone's Charge," described the event as including "800 men of Weisiger's Brigade" and "composed mainly of Petersburg men."[25]

The Park Service wasted no time using the Crater to attract people to the park. On April 30, 1937, a reenactment was held for an estimated 50,000 spectators. An immense amount of planning and publicity work was required, and during the month preceding the reenactment, park employees devoted most of their time to the affair. Preparations included the construction of a stand, an enclosure for invited guests, six latrines, two enclosures for the press, two structures to represent bombproofs, temporary imitation earthworks, and battery positions. Workers went to great lengths to create a realistic visual scene for the audience; monuments on the fields were camouflaged, and arrangements were made to prohibit airplanes from flying over the area during the day.[26]

The *Richmond Times-Dispatch* reported to its readers that they could "see reproduced the greatest fiasco in modern warfare." Once again the attention would be on Mahone's brigade; those in attendance would see how Mahone's men "came to reinforce the Crater's defenders and how they dashed into the Crater themselves, screaming the Rebel yell, goaded to insane fury by the faces of a Negro division Burnside had thrown into

(*Above*) An estimated 50,000 spectators attended the 1937 Crater reenactment, which included the detonation of a thirty-eight-pound charge. (*Richmond Times-Dispatch*, May 1, 1937)

(*Below*) Nearly 3,000 troops, including 650 Virginia Military Institute cadets and 1,200 Marines, played the roles of the combatants in the reenactment that took place on April 30, 1937. (*Richmond Times-Dispatch*, May 1, 1937)

the fight." Six thousand seats for spectators were sold for 50¢, though general admission and parking came with no charge.[27]

A total of nearly 3,000 troops, including 650 Virginia Military Institute cadets and 1,200 Marines, played the roles of the combatants. Not surprisingly, no effort was made to represent the role African Americans played in the battle. Rehearsals took place on April 30 to ensure accuracy; a thirty-eight-pound charge was exploded in imitation of the mine explosion that had signaled the start of the battle. For the Marines, the "sham battle" was an opportunity to finally play the role of the victors: "They obligingly have met defeat in their role of Union troops in several previous Virginia reenactments of battles of the '60's." Preparations also benefited from programs in Franklin Roosevelt's New Deal. Replicas of the flags carried into battle were made by women in the Works Progress Administration, many of whom were descendants of participants in the battle, and camps for the reenactors were constructed by the Civilian Conservation Corps.[28]

Ticket holders received a program reproducing John Elder's famous painting of the Crater and providing a short history of the battle. Celebrations commenced with an opening address by Congressman Drewry, who introduced several of the prominent guests, including Virginia's governor George C. Perry. Douglas S. Freeman provided historical background to the events of July 30, 1864, and with the help of an amplifying system pointed out landmarks on the battlefield. The reenactment was divided into two stages. The first, including a dialogue authored by Freeman, re-created the conversation among Union commanders in the final hours before the attack. Freeman's narrative foreshadows the failed attack by emphasizing the disappointment of Union commanders upon learning that General Ferrero's division of black soldiers would not be taking the lead in the assault. Ferrero comments, "They're trained for it, thoroughly; they know every move." The other generals express grave doubt that such a last-minute change can succeed. The first stage concluded with the timed explosion and Union attack, ending in a "confused mass of men in the crater." Around 3:00 p.m. the second phase kicked off with the "arrival of Weisiger's Brigade of Mahone's Confederate Division" and ended with the surrender of Union troops.[29]

Only four men from Mahone's brigade were in attendance; one was ninety-three-year-old Francis M. Ridout of Petersburg. Invitations to Union veterans who took part in the battle went out, but none attended

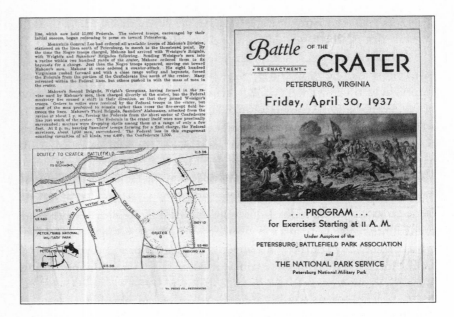

The April 30, 1937, Crater reenactment marked the inclusion of the battlefield within the boundaries of the new military park. John Elder's famous painting of Mahone's charge graced the cover of the program. (Author's collection)

owing to age. Park officials judged the reenactment a success and were especially pleased that little damage had been done to the grounds. Franklin W. Smith, president of the Petersburg Battlefield Park Association, believed "it was one of the greatest things ever held in Petersburg." Two days later, a Petersburg paper reported that one army officer still "has not gotten over his thrill of witnessing the reenactment." M. Clifford Harrison waxed poetic in his brief reference to the reenactment written a few years later. Harrison recalled "a spontaneous Rebel yell" from the crowd as Weisiger's men approached the point of their famous charge: "We couldn't have repressed our Southern emotions at that moment if we had wanted to. Our yell was the voice of the South reverberating down three-quarters of a century."[30]

The day before the reenactment, an editorial appeared in the *Richmond Times-Dispatch* expressing concern over the upcoming event. The writer believed that it would be unfortunate if the National Park Service's goal were to "impress onlookers with the feeling that war is glamorous or in any sense an alluring spectacle. We hope the lesson to be learned from it," continued the writer, "will be that we of this generation must avoid such an experience." While the collective memory of the Crater on display in the 1937 reenactment was not "glamorous," it was a wholly celebratory remembrance of the bravery of William Mahone and his Virginia brigade. The success of Jim Crow in Virginia was clearly discerned in the absence of any serious attention to the presence of black soldiers, and it is likely the case that very few, if any, local African Americans attended. The black community's inability to contribute to local Civil War memory was now compounded by the National Park Service's inheritance of a narrative that it could exploit to increase revenue by attracting tourists from around the country.[31]

Chapter 6

COMPETING MEMORIES
Civil War and Civil Rights

IN THE TWO decades after World War II, American families took to the roads on vacations that had as much to do with pleasure as with a desire to explore historic sites that reflected the country's national identity and democratic values. In 1954 alone, around 49 million Americans set out on heritage tours of the United States, including Mount Vernon, Gettysburg, Washington, D.C., and Independence Hall. These sacred places connected Americans with a rich history that allowed them to imagine themselves members of a larger community bound together by common values. Such a connection with history and heritage encouraged good citizenship at the height of America's ideological struggle against the Soviet Union.[1]

Although Petersburg was certainly not as popular as Gettysburg, Fredericksburg, and Antietam, families did make it a vacation destination or at least stopped briefly to tour specific sites such as the Crater. Tours of the eastern front of the Petersburg campaign began at Battery 5 and ended at the Crater. Visitors learned about the battle through the physical landscape, which included earthworks in various stages of preservation as well as a series of wayside markers and exhibits. Battery 5 included a trailside exhibit that described the initial Union assaults in June 1864 as well as three thirty-pound Parrot rifles. A representative of the National Park Service at the Crater met visitors, and further information was made available. Visitors could survey additional examples of field artillery tubes, view a small number of exhibits in a field museum, and purchase postcards, including a reproduction of John Elder's famous painting of the battle, from a vending machine. The park also offered a well-laid path to the entrance and remains of the mine as well as the crater itself. By this time the landscape, beyond what little remained of the actual hole, had lost most of its wartime character owing to the brief existence of the golf course and park service maintenance.[2]

The wayside markers as well as the guide's interpretation of the Crater and broader campaign followed the standard story that had taken shape by the time the National Park Service took control of the site. Emphasis was placed on the strategic importance of the city and the evolution of the campaign as well as on the drama of the construction of the tunnel and preparations for the Union assault. Visitors were treated to a vivid description of the explosion and a broad outline of the battle itself in all of its horrific detail. Finally, William Mahone's counterattack was acknowledged as the dramatic turning point of the morning's fighting. In all of this, Americans learned little about the crucial role that African Americans played in this battle or of the event's overall significance in the war after 1863. The literature available at this time offered very little to assist visitors in better understanding the experiences of black soldiers, and the lack of intent to highlight their contribution to the battle made it unlikely that visitors learned anything about the slaughter of these men following the battle.

The battle and the war as a whole, presented thus devoid of any political and social context, reflected an understanding that many American families brought with them to the battlefield, and it was validation of this narrative that they were looking to connect with. Any attempt to provide additional information about the presence of African American soldiers and their treatment at the hands of outraged Confederates would have challenged a consensus view that few Americans were prepared to confront. What visitors could not know was that events on the racial front, beginning with the Supreme Court's landmark ruling in *Brown v. Board of Education,* would, in a few short years, challenge America's collective memory of the war and its fundamental meaning. These challenges eventually led to substantive changes in the way the National Park Service interpreted the Petersburg campaign and the Crater. How visitors experience the park today is reflective of these significant changes.

The 1937 reenactment brought a version of the Crater story to a new generation gearing up for another world war. Compared with the 1903 reenactment, little had changed in the way the landscape of the Crater was interpreted. The establishment of the Petersburg National Military Park—and the uncritical acceptance by its research staff of an interpreta-

tion that downplayed race and highlighted the virtues of national reunion—all but guaranteed that visitors would receive a skewed account of
the events of July 30, 1864. To a great extent veterans on both sides shaped
the way in which the landscape would be interpreted by future generations. Neither side had any interest in reminding the other of the important role black soldiers played in the battle, nor did they raise questions of
responsibility or blame for the causes of the war. Without any reference to
broader issues of race or questions involving the reasons for the war, the
landscape was understood strictly in military terms involving the movement of soldiers—if only of one color. In short, the battlefield became a
symbol of shared values, a monument to the sacrifice of veterans on both
sides, supported by the government and the American people.

During the two decades after the 1937 reenactment, the Park Service
worked to develop its interpretive facilities in order to continue to attract
crowds to the battlefields around Petersburg. The clubhouse that had once
housed the Crater Battlefield Association was converted into a museum,
and an eleven-foot-square relief map of the entire Petersburg siege was
installed for the benefit of visitors. In addition, an amplified six-minute
recording was mounted in a tree at the Crater, which offered an overview
of the battle for visitors as they walked the remains, including the tunnel
and other intact fortifications within the battle site. By 1939 there were
thirty-five temporary 100-word markers placed along the driving tour
route at such sites as Battery Five, Fort Stedman, and the Crater; permanent markers along with self-guided tours of Fort Wadsworth and Battery
5 later replaced these signs. After World War II, an ordnance exhibit of
eighteen pieces of artillery was added to the Crater site, including a Coe-
horn mortar, a thirty-two-pounder naval gun, and a twelve-pounder
breech-loading Whitworth rifle.[3]

While the Park Service worked vigorously to improve the physical
plant and access to sites such as the Crater, little changed in terms of how
the battle itself was interpreted. All the improvements reinforced strictly
military aspects of the battle, specifically the initial mine explosion and
the role of Virginians, including William Mahone and the Virginia brigade of David Weisiger. As a result, visitation to the Petersburg battlefields
increased from roughly 150,000 in 1938 to 215,000 in 1955. The superintendent of the park reported optimistically in 1938 that "a review of the
monthly summary of registrations reveals that most of the states are represented each month, along with numerous visitors from other countries."

Students at the mine leading to the tunnel to the Crater, ca. 1937–1946. The Crater proved to be an attractive destination for Virginia's white student population, but very few African Americans traveled to the battlefield, given the interpretation of the battle that had evolved by this time. (P-990, Petersburg Museums)

In addition to the general public, the Crater also attracted the attention of visitors from the Army War College, a group of Washington professionals who styled themselves the "Battlefield Crackpates," and numerous military officers from such countries as Greece, England, France, and Germany. In April 1946, General and Mrs. Dwight D. Eisenhower toured the battlefields around Petersburg.[4]

The concentration on improving the physical landscape of the Crater up to and through World War II reinforced an already deeply ingrained interpretation of the battle that highlighted the widely held values of bravery and leadership in the face of unspeakable horrors. Newspapers referenced speeches and publications about the Crater from the turn of the century that implored their audiences to honor "the places where these memorable acts were done," where "American generals led brave American soldiers in a series of great battles," and thus all "may be inspired by the courage and heroism they displayed." Park literature continued this trend through World War II. A small guide published in 1942 characterized the park's mission as one that "commemorates the valor and devotion of the American soldiers who served around Petersburg during the Revolution and the War Between the States." The fighting in Europe and the Pacific provided another opportunity to remind visitors of the "new era in the history of America" that emerged out of the Civil War. In 1950 the Park Service published a fifty-six-page booklet titled *Petersburg Battlefields* authored by Richard W. Lykes, which provided even more detailed coverage of the campaign. The ten pages devoted to the Crater focused in detail on the construction and explosion of the mine followed by the standard outline of the battle. Apart from referencing the South Carolina brigade that had been caught in the explosion, Lykes concentrated on Mahone's counterattack and the conduct of the Virginia brigade. Not surprisingly, Lykes makes no reference to the slaughter of black soldiers following their surrender.[5]

The educational value of the Petersburg battlefields was stressed early on as a way to attract visitors and forge connections with school districts around the Commonwealth. As early as 1934, research technician Branch Spalding described the sites as a "potential educational instrument." As the *Petersburg Progress-Index* reported, however, the educational staff outlined an agenda that fell in line with the Park Service's overall interpretation:

> The possibility of making teaching more effective was stressed by him [Spalding] in his explanation of the field and park museum, for they will offer to pupils and teachers more about the siege of Petersburg, the beginning of modern warfare and other things than can be secured in books alone. He showed how the park can be helpful in the study of geography, in history, economics, botany and animal life. The importance of streams, of bridges and ravines in the history of the nine-month siege of Petersburg and all warfare was shown too, by Mr. Spalding in an interesting series of six timed maps of the Battle of the Crater. Such maps will be part of the educational features of the museums, giving the locations of troops and their movements at specific times.

This narrow focus left no room for any meaningful analysis of how the presence of USCTs during the battle connected to the broader issues of race and emancipation during the Civil War. There is very little reference to any park contact with black schools in the Petersburg area beyond a visit by thirty-two students from the Franklin County (colored) Training

School in April 1937. The park's records indicate a single meeting of the Negro Masons in September 1938.[6]

On July 3, 1956, the Petersburg National Military Park celebrated its thirtieth anniversary with an "Establishment Day" ceremony in the visitor center, which was to be formally dedicated as part of the program. The principal speaker was Franklin W. Smith, whose service as the president of the Petersburg Battlefield Park stretched back to 1926. Smith offered enthusiastic remarks about the hard work carried out to improve the physical layout and interpretive services of Petersburg's battlefields; his "treasured" map of the grounds showed clearly the amount of land acquired by the federal government, from 346 acres in 1926 to 1,505.44 acres. Although speakers generally reflected on the past, the ceremony also offered the opportunity to discuss a new long-term plan aimed at improving every park in the system.[7]

The most significant development was the Department of the Interior's authorization of the Mission 66 Development Program, which brought specific improvements to the Petersburg parks, including a new visitor center that was completed in May 1967 and increased access through roads and bridges. A new interpretive program that included additional audio stations and a ten-stop tour that began at Battery 5 and ended at the Crater was also created. The additional audio stations supplemented those already being utilized at Fort Stedman and the Crater; two more were set up at the tunnel entrance, and another described the Confederate counterattacks. The broader goal of Mission 66—as it related to the park's Civil War battlefields—was to prepare the sites for the large crowds expected in connection with the nation's Civil War centennial celebrations, which would run from 1961 to 1965.[8]

Americans were exuberant at the prospect of the upcoming Civil War centennial celebrations. In 1957 Congress authorized the Civil War Centennial Commission, choosing Ulysses S. Grant III to serve as its chairman. With the help of Karl S. Betts, a former advertising executive who served as executive director, the commission hoped to tap into this centennial excitement by concentrating on the shared values that had come to define the nation's collective memory of the war by emphasizing sectional reconciliation and the bravery of the men who fought on both sides—and by avoiding potential controversy. The centennial offered Americans a chance to unfurl Confederate battle flags and ponder the character and heroism of such iconic figures as Robert E. Lee and Thomas "Stonewall"

A few monuments can be found at the Crater. This crowd (ca. 1932–1946) stands next to a monument to the Second Pennsylvania Heavy Artillery, and a monument to William Mahone can be seen in the background. (Petersburg Museums)

Jackson. Families could watch as reenactors brought to life memorable battles such as First Manassas and Gettysburg, where lessons could be taught about the common bonds of bravery and patriotism that most white Americans had come to believe had animated the men on both sides.[9]

In 1955 the Virginia Civil War Centennial, Inc., was given a corporate charter by the Commonwealth to organize events that would commemorate some of the bloodiest engagements of the war. The organization's preliminary plan, authored by Charles T. Moses, echoed the themes of reconciliation and patriotism that defined the work of the national commission:

The Civil War Centennial is a commemorative effort of greater magnitude than any ever before undertaken by the Commonwealth of Virginia. The Virginia Civil War Commission's plans are designed to interpret and explain this cataclysmic period of history to our own people and those who visit us and to call attention to the heroism, the idealism and the devotion to principle displayed during the War. The Commission hopes that a theme of moral and spiritual regeneration will run through all of its activities. Virginia has an opportunity to attract millions of out-of-state visitors through an exciting Centennial program. But Virginia has an even greater opportunity to inspire these people to be as dedicated to great ideals in a time of peace as our forbears were in a time of war. This is the time for Virginia to emphasize the victory of character won by Lee and others in rising above the horrors of war and the shame of defeat.[10]

In a publication made available to Virginia's teachers, the commission suggested that "the Centennial is no time for finding fault or placing blame or fighting the issues all over again." Blame for the war could be found on all sides. According to the manual, the deep divisions that spawned the war "grew out of hate, greed and fear, ignorance and apathy, selfishness and emotionalism—evils from which this generation is not free." Teachers were instructed to impart to their students a dramatic narrative of the war by concentrating on the soldiers and the battlefield as well as on the broad themes of "Heroes and Patriotism." Not surprisingly, Robert E. Lee stood out as the central figure of the war: "Lee's words should have as much meaning to Virginians today as they did in reconstruction times."[11]

Individual counties and cities organized their own committees, which reported to the state commission. In Petersburg, Richard T. Wilson III, chairman of the city's committee, set out to promote a small slate of activities beginning with an opening ceremony to honor the centennial along with a parade and rededication program. A "camera club" contest was also designed to furnish slides of area sites for the local committee. Not surprisingly, the Crater battlefield was singled out for attention, and the local committee pledged to cooperate with the National Park Service to commemorate the 100th anniversary of the battle. A reflection of its popularity was clearly visible in a brochure published by the Petersburg Chamber of Commerce in 1961. The brochure featured Elder's famous painting on the cover and advertised the city as the "birthplace of total war." It is unknown whether those involved planned a reenactment of the battle, but given the popularity of the two previous events, in 1903 and 1937, it is likely that the subject was discussed.[12]

Even as Americans geared up for celebration, however, problems festered just below the surface. The growing civil rights movement presented a direct challenge to the way white Americans wished to remember the war by highlighting continued racial injustice as a result of the unfinished business of the Civil War and Reconstruction. As much as white Americans wanted to celebrate and remember their preferred interpretation of the war, the continued problem of race served as a reminder that not all was well. Indeed, the images of Lee and Jackson were being challenged on a daily basis by the names of Martin L. King, Rosa Parks, Medgar Evers, and Emmett Till, as well as by news of school desegregation, lunch counter sit-ins, and Freedom Riders. The civil rights movement presented a challenge to centennial event organizers and participants by casting a shadow on the nation's self-proclaimed status as the leader of the free world at the height of the cold war.

By 1960 the nation had witnessed violence and protest following the 1954 Supreme Court case *Brown v. Board of Education* and school desegregation along with the Montgomery bus boycott in Alabama. In the spring of that year, in an effort to desegregate department store lunch counters, students staged sit-ins beginning in Greensboro, North Carolina, and within a short period of time 115 stores had been integrated in over 100 cities, including four national chains. While individual protestors and organizations may have been focused narrowly on "the prize" of basic civil rights, their collective actions served to turn the centennial celebrations into a contested landscape where the accepted historical narrative could be challenged and revised.[13]

The decision of the Civil War Centennial Commission to hold its annual assembly in the city of Charleston, South Carolina, in April 1961 as part of the commemoration of the attack on Fort Sumter set the tone for the challenges that would be faced throughout the four years of commemoration. Segregation policies in Charleston meant that black commission members from Northern states would not be able to stay at the Francis Marion Hotel. A public relations fiasco was avoided with a last-minute decision and assistance by the Kennedy administration to move the proceedings to a federal military facility outside Charleston.[14]

The reenactment of First Manassas that took place in July 1961 reflected the growing racial divide between the struggle for civil rights and the centennial even more clearly. Reenactments proved to be the most controversial forms of commemoration; in addition to the cost and difficulties associated with preparation, national commission leaders were skeptical that they could accurately depict the horror of the battlefield. This did not stop organizers from scheduling a three-day event, and while investors failed to earn a profit, it did attract over 3,000 reenactors and an audience that numbered over 100,000. Critics of the purely celebratory and one-sided character of these events could not help but draw a connection between the moral high ground of the Freedom Riders who were viciously attacked in Alabama and the celebratory tone of the centennial. "The war was in vain, the celebration is a blasphemy and a disgrace," wrote Rabbi Bernard Bamberger on June 20, 1961, "if a century later the Negro's right to full equality may still be limited by prejudice enacted into law or perpetuated by custom." The sight of thousands of white Southerners waving Confederate flags and shouting the "rebel yell" following the defeat of Union troops on the battlefield only fueled the revulsion of black Americans and other critics.[15]

The response by African Americans to the Manassas reenactment was part of a much broader critique of the centennial. In May 1961 African American historian Lawrence D. Reddick, who had recently been fired from his post at Alabama State College in Montgomery for comments in support of civil rights, addressed a group of teachers in New York City urging them to resist the myth making that was being used by centennial planners to challenge those who were pushing for civil rights. Reddick went on to ask President Kennedy to issue a statement calling on black Americans to honor the centennial with a critical eye. The veteran civil rights and labor leader A. Philip Randolph was even more direct: "There is no doubt that this whole Civil War Centennial commemoration is a stupendous brain-washing exercise to make the Civil War leaders of the South on par with the Civil War leaders of the North, and to strike a blow against men of color and human dignity." The authors of a pamphlet published by the Vanguard Society of America echoed Randolph's sentiments: centennial planners had set out to do nothing less than "to build up the Dixiecrats, to put billions of new dollars into their hands, to offset civil rights gains in the South and to destroy the broad mass movement for Negro-white unity for civil rights."[16]

As part of their critical assessment of the centennial, African Americans offered a robust counter-memory of the Civil War that highlighted the importance of slavery in bringing about secession and war, a bottom-up narrative that emphasized their own roles as full historical agents in achieving their freedom as well as the sacrifice and heroism of black soldiers on the battlefield. Popular accounts of USCTs benefited from the scholarship of Benjamin Quarles and Dudley T. Cornish, both of whom published important studies in the 1950s. Focus on these soldiers not only worked to correct the historical record, it forged strong connections between those who had fought and died for freedom in the 1860s and those who were struggling to gain the fruits of that freedom a century later.[17]

Scholarly work was filtered down to the black American middle class through newspapers and popular magazines. The *Richmond Afro-American* offered its readers a continual stream of articles focusing on a wide range of subjects relating to black contributions to the Civil War, especially the history of USCTs in Virginia. In early 1961 an article appeared criticizing a series of essays written by popular historian Bruce Catton, which the author believed failed to account for the role "played by colored Africans." The author corrected this oversight by referencing some of the earliest attempts to recruit black men into the Union army as well as the role of Frederick Douglass in convincing Lincoln of the need to utilize this untapped source. "Their fight was for freedom and against an enemy," asserted this writer, reminding readers that the enemy "gave no quarter to white officers or troops in colored regiments." That the newspaper's offices were located in the former capital of the Confederacy also offered ample opportunity to remind readers of the abandonment of Richmond on April 2, 1865, and of the celebrations that ensued when USCTs entered the city.[18]

Arguably, many African Americans learned about the Civil War in the pages of *Ebony* and *Jet*. Both magazines strove to encourage a new political and historical consciousness among their readers by relating the actions of black Civil War soldiers. *Ebony* commissioned Lerone Bennett Jr. to write a series of articles on black history, including a June 1962 essay titled, "The Negro in the Civil War." Bennett would later become known for his harsh critique of Lincoln's racial outlook and of the steps that led to the issuing of the Emancipation Proclamation. Bennett stressed the steps that ordinary African Americans took to win their freedom and offered a thorough overview of the battles that USCTs took part in, including the Crater. Well-known lithographs depicting black soldiers in battle usually accompanied such articles, and one issue of *Ebony* published in 1968 featured on its cover black men in the military uniforms of previous American wars. Although early 1960s' articles addressing the history of

African American service in the Union army left readers with a sense of optimism about the past and present, the escalation of the war in Vietnam and growing tensions on the racial front left some doubting the possibility of real change. The past, after all, was in some respects dispiriting. "When the Civil War ended," asserted one editorial, "black soldiers found that they had moved up just one small notch." While they enjoyed the benefits of legal citizenship as a result of the Fourteenth and Fifteenth amendments, their lack of work and empty pockets meant that "they had exchanged legal slavery for economic slavery."[19]

For many readers, the history lessons were nothing less than an awakening. Writing from Brooklyn, Marie Josey lamented the fact that *Ebony* was not being read by more white Americans. While Josey was disturbed by the tendency of whites to think of "Negroes [as]'docile' slaves," she admitted that "this was my conception of the Negro until I started subscribing to your magazine." Others, like James E. Haynes of Cleveland, honed in on the feelings of empowerment that these stories engendered, writing that they "lend encouragement and moral support to our stride-breaking brothers in the South." Published letters suggest that, indeed, the majority of readers lived in Northern states. Even though this region experienced significant racial upheaval throughout this time, the focus of the articles on the Civil War South allowed Northern black readers to identify more closely with hardships elsewhere.[20]

Jet magazine also kept readers apprised of centennial events, even offering commentary that challenged the way the war was being commemorated, but its history features were more subdued compared to *Ebony*. A regular column featured key moments in the Civil War, including the expected list of battles in which USCTs fought. The charge of the Fourth Division at the Crater was described as a "gallant" one that would have succeeded if not for the failure of "Federal support." Human-interest stories such as Rev. Herman White's application to the Veterans Administration for "war bonuses" owed to three ancestors who fought in the Civil War served as a lesson to readers that they could empower themselves and uncover a personal connection to ancestors who fought through accessing documents available in the National Archives.[21]

For young civil rights activists like Frank Smith, who would later establish the African American Civil War Museum in Washington, D.C., the introduction to the history of USCTs occurred while organizing voter registration drives in Mississippi during this period. Meeting a descendant of a USCT highlighted the "contradiction between the lack of civil rights among blacks today with the sacrifices made by black men during the Civil War." Over the next few years Smith nurtured a close connection between civil rights activism and history while attending college in Mississippi, where he was introduced to the scholarly work of Cornish, Quarrels, and John Hope Franklin.[22]

While white Americans' interest in the centennial declined as a result of events on the political and racial front, the NAACP, the Association for the Study of Negro Life and History, founded by Carter G. Woodson in 1915, and other black organizations stepped up their attacks in 1963 by asserting their own black counter-memory of the centennial of the Emancipation Proclamation, continuing to make use of stories about armed black soldiers. The *Crisis* boldly argued that the proclamation was the culmination of a process that "finally finished opening the door that Thomas Wentworth Higginson's pioneer regiment had pried loose in the Sea Islands of South Carolina." Howard Meyer went on to chastise the public school system for failing to educate students on the important role that USCTs had played in maintaining the Union and ending slavery. He also criticized the historical profession, which he believed continued to intentionally ignore this subject. Articles about black soldiers found in the pages of the *Crisis* during the centennial of the Emancipation Proclamation were as much about "integrating America's heritage" as they were about emphasizing that African Americans had through their own actions demonstrated that the "Negro race deserved to be free."[23]

This resurgence of interest in the contributions of African Americans in the Civil War eventually filtered down to a limited number of classrooms across the country. Publications such as the *Negro History Bulletin* and new textbooks encouraged students to take pride in their collective past and an interest in the centennial. Observance of Negro History Week throughout this period included numerous appeals to students to remember that "Negro soldiers who wore the Union blue" made up "ten per cent of the total army." These "Freedom Lessons" tended to offer a more moderate message, encouraging young black Americans to identify with and even to revere the nation's democratic institutions and "the ideals of America."[24]

Regardless of the Kennedy administration's lackluster performance in the area of civil rights legislation, black and white activists continued to challenge the limits of the nation's racial tolerance as well as ongoing centennial events. While King marched on Washington, D.C., in July 1963, crowds gathered at Gettysburg to remember the "High Water-Mark." In contrast to the crowd that had witnessed the "rebel yell" back in July 1961 at Manassas, audiences at Gettysburg witnessed a contest for control of the meaning of the battle. Governor George Wallace of Alabama used the occasion to deliver a states' rights address next to a monument to Alabamians who fought in the battle. Northern governors from Pennsylvania and New Jersey countered that the war was fought to end slavery and that the battle's dead could not rest until full political rights were granted to every American.

The centennial anniversary of Lincoln's Emancipation Proclamation proved difficult to control as critics pointed out the wide gulf between the promise of freedom and the present reality. The editors of the journal *Freedomways* predicted that "the world will take note of the fact that the system of segregation and discrimination continues to deprive some 20 million Negro Americans of their rightful status as citizens in the political, economic and social life of the nation one hundred years after slavery's end was decreed by President Abraham Lincoln." In addition to the introduction of emancipation, other significant events, including the assassination of President Kennedy in November 1963, the civil rights agenda of Lyndon B. Johnson's administration (which culminated in the Voting Rights Act of 1964), and the nation's growing involvement in Vietnam alienated even more white Americans from taking part in centennial events.[25]

By 1964 centennial organizers in Petersburg were forced to acknowledge that the general public that had lost interest in commemorating the Civil War as well as more dramatic changes in the racial and political structure of the city. The population of Petersburg in 1960 was approximately 19,000 whites and 17,000 African Americans and yet, as in many Southern cities, the former controlled local political power. Beginning in 1960 Petersburg erupted in civil rights demonstrations that continued throughout the decade. Leadership from area churches such as Gillfield Baptist Church, led by Rev. Wyatt Tee Walker, the local chapter of the NAACP, and area schools such as Virginia State College, with its rich history stemming back to its founding during the Readjuster era, all worked to encourage and support the protest movement.[26]

The early flashpoint for organized protest in Petersburg was the desegregation of the city's William R. McKenney Central Library, formerly the home of William Mahone after the Civil War. The segregated library restricted black patrons' access to resources by forcing them to use a side entrance and a poorly lit basement. The remaining floors and library stacks were reserved for whites. Led by the Reverends Walker and R. G. Williams, 140 demonstrators from Virginia State College and Peabody High School took seats on the first two floors of the library on February 27, 1960. Walker approached the counter of Petersburg's central library and asked for a biography of General Robert E. Lee written by Douglas Southall Freeman. In response, the library closed for four days to all patrons, and the city council, despite pleas to end library segregation, passed a strict anti-trespassing ordinance to discourage protests. On March 17, fifteen black patrons entered the library's front door and took seats, which led to the arrest of eleven.[27]

Following the sit-in, protests spread to other public sites, including the Blue Bird Theater and the Trailways Bus Terminal Restaurant, which was forced to desegregate on August 15. A series of visits by Martin Luther King Jr. led to voter drives throughout the city and helped to maintain pressure on the city council. The following May a group of Freedom Riders disembarked at the very same terminal and were hosted overnight without incident. By 1964 activists had registered voters, challenged biased hiring practices and, most important, prepared the way for the inclusion of African Americans in positions of civic authority. That same year the first African American was elected to Petersburg's city council.[28]

The combination of social and political unrest in the city, along with broader national trends, dampened enthusiasm for an elaborate commemoration of the battle of the Crater. Those committed to remembering the war had to deal not only with the theme of emancipation and fewer Confederate victories to celebrate but also with the recruitment of black Americans into the Union army, their introduction to the fighting in 1864, and unpleasant episodes such as the massacre at Fort Pillow. Given these conditions, the lack of any concerted effort to draw attention to a battle that highlighted many of the themes now being emphasized within the black community is understandable. While the 1903 and 1937 reenactments had been able to easily steer clear of the divisive issues of emancipation and race, the racial unrest in Petersburg and changes to local government would have made it unlikely that organizers could pull off an event that celebrated white Virginians and ignored the presence of USCTs. Indeed, a large-scale ceremony commemorating the Crater would have been an ideal event for individuals and organizations interested in introducing a black counter-memory to remember emancipation, honor the contributions of African Americans, and draw connections to the on-going civil rights struggle.

While it can be easily explained why the Petersburg Civil War Centennial Commission resisted organizing a reenactment, what is remarkable is just how little was done to mark the 100th anniversary of the Crater. Even without a reenactment, other examples of pageantry would have been possible, including flag presentations, infantry drill, and even parades of soldiers in Civil War uniform. The ceremony that did take place involved little more than the formal dedication of a small marker commemorating the battle presented by Petersburg mayor Marvin W. Gill Jr. on behalf of the people of the city to the Petersburg National Battlefield Park. Most newspaper accounts of the ceremony were relatively brief; in addition to providing a basic outline of the ceremony, they mentioned that the Park Service was planning to restore the entrance to the tunnel.

The lack of enthusiasm for the monument dedication was borne out in an editorial that had appeared the day before. The author was relegated to having to remind his readers that "cognizance should be taken of the best known event which occurred in Petersburg during its ordeal of 1864–65 and indeed during the long span of the community's history." The writer admitted that residents of the city could "plead innocent" to "having a burning interest" in centennial events and that he himself "felt apologetic about our whole performance." In conclusion, the writer struggled to find a sufficient reason for the public to attend the commemoration at all: "As a matter of fact, there are some people who are interested whether they have some sentimental concern or simply feel that good citizenship requires an awareness of the past, present, and future of a community. No one of these three reasons should be excluded." Newspaper photographs show a small number of people in attendance.[29]

By not holding an elaborate commemorative ceremony, interested parties sought to protect their preferred interpretation of the battle that celebrated the heroism of white Confederates, primarily from Mahone's Virginia brigade. A decision to hold a more prominent event would have invited challenges to the way public memory of the battle had been used so effectively to reinforce white political control of the state by ignoring the steps that African Americans had taken during the Civil War to secure their own freedom and civil rights.

Centennial events continued into 1965, but the crowds were small and their enthusiasm diminished as both domestic and foreign issues took center stage. Confederate flags had been unfurled, but they now stood atop Southern state capital buildings, not simply as a symbol of "Massive Resistance" but also as a defense of a past that had come under increasing attack. While most civil rights activists between 1961 and 1965 concentrated on the more immediate goal of political empowerment rather than on challenging popular perceptions of the Civil War, their actions would lead in the decades to follow to significant changes in the historical landscape.

In 1967 Travis J. L. Stephens completed an M.A. thesis at Virginia State College (now University) on USCTs at the Crater. Relying heavily on the small body of scholarship that kept the history of this subject alive within academic circles, the thesis offered a detailed tactical account of the Fourth Division during the battle. Stephens strays from his military focus only a few times, but toward the end of his work he offers an assessment that, read in the context of Petersburg in 1967, suggests a perspective that extends beyond 1865: "One need no longer question the ability of the Negro to fight, for at each of the battles described, he not only fought, but died valiantly." The completion of such a thesis in close proximity to the Crater battlefield at this point in time suggests that a new generation of African Americans had discovered Civil War history and pointed to the possibility of renewing Petersburg's Civil War heritage within the black community.[30]

Chapter 7

MOVING FORWARD

Integrating a Black Counter-Memory

IN 1974 THE Petersburg National Battlefield (PNB) placed a marker at Battery Nine, along the driving tour, to acknowledge its capture by US-CTs on June 15, 1864. At about the same time, residents of Petersburg learned that their battlefields had been included, along with twelve other historical sites, as National Historical Landmarks with a connection to black history. Other signs of change could be seen on the battlefield as well. Superintendent Larry Hakel indicated that the staff would redouble its efforts to interpret the battlefields so as to reflect the participation of black soldiers. Visual changes could be seen as well with the inclusion of two black interpreters in the park's Living History program. One of the two was Henry Branch, a history major at Shaw University in Raleigh, North Carolina. "Many of the visitors tell me," said Branch, that "I am the first black they have seen involved in living history presentations." Regrettably, he noted, "Some, when I get to the part blacks played in the Civil War, turn and walk away."[1]

The challenges faced by the PNB in the 1970s had much in common with those faced by other public and private historical institutions, such as Colonial Williamsburg, the John Brown House, Monticello, and countless historic plantation homes that dealt with the tough questions of how to interpret slavery and race. Although the limited number of scholarly studies was in part to blame, more practical problems included limits on finances, scarcity of artifacts that reflected the African American and USCT experience in Petersburg, and sparse attendance by black Americans.[2]

By the end of the 1970s, and particularly after the release of Alex Haley's *Roots: The Saga of an American Family* in 1976, it was becoming much more difficult to fend off challenges and discontent from those who visited historical sites and found the coverage of black history seriously lacking. Haley's popular miniseries' portrayal of African Americans as full historical agents revealed a richer history that had been hidden behind years of white control of historical sites. African Americans who went looking for their story at some of the nation's most cherished historical locations must have been sorely disappointed. For a growing number of people, however, that disappointment translated into action.[3]

The popular diffusion of a narrative more sympathetic to the experiences of African Americans during the Civil War was aided by continued advances in the scholarship of slavery as well as of the military history of the Civil War. Historians of slavery continued to uncover the myriad ways in which the actions of slaves, on the plantation, in contraband camps, and eventually in the army itself, contributed to Union victory while military historians broadened their understanding of battles and campaigns to include the experiences of noncombatants. Such scholarship opened up opportunities not only to challenge many deeply ingrained institutional narratives but to suggest ways to supplement and enrich those stories as well.[4]

The most concerted challenge to the PNB took place in 1978, when a group from Howard University, led by Professor Joseph E. Harris, visited to survey the steps taken to explain the history of black Americans in the city of Petersburg as well as in the Petersburg campaign. The team looked specifically at how well the National Park Service had integrated this black history into its overall interpretation of the battlefields. The final report clearly reflected the damage done as a result of the sanitization of the Civil War over the course of the twentieth century and offered a specific set of recommendations to begin to correct this oversight.

The report begins on an optimistic note: the "Petersburg National Battlefield is an excellent site to illustrate the contributions of black personnel during the Civil War." Since both the Union and Confederate sides had used the services of blacks, park officials would be able to include exhibits that reflected the "various occupations in which slaves and freedmen were employed." To achieve this goal, however, specific steps were recommended. Interviews with park employees revealed how little information about the black experience during the Petersburg campaign was shared with visitors. While some rangers showed interest in the story of black soldiers at the Crater, others were unaware of their participation in the battles or of the support roles played by slaves and free blacks. According to the report, some employees assumed a defensive posture, refusing to share what information was available about USCTs when the general public asked questions. The lack of black personnel was also of concern to the research team, as the PNB "has never had more than a few black employees" and those who had been hired were in positions other than as guides and interpreters. The report recommended that black employees be hired on a three-year cycle, though it did reference the attempt to hire interns from Virginia State College.[5]

The most revealing section of the report touches on how local black students at Virginia State College felt about the way in which the National Park Service presented the battle to the public. According to college archivist Lucious Edwards, "The students are offended by the sympathetic presentation which glorifies the southern counterattack against the black soldiers at the Crater, while previous exploits of black soldiers are dismissed in a few words." The students, continued Edwards, "consider the primary function of Petersburg National Battlefield as maintaining or glorifying the image of the Confederacy" and were left with the unfortunate impression "that local white residents view the park as their own personal recreation area and that blacks have only a token Negro's heritage in a negative setting." On a more practical level, the research team suggested that the PNB supplement its library and books for purchase to include studies of the African American experience. "PNB publications present very little information about black soldiers," the report continued, "and nothing about their interest in the Petersburg campaign." The report concluded: "The Petersburg campaign, including the Battle of the Crater, is an excellent theme to incorporate the significance of black personnel during the Civil War. In this campaign, black troops were used in enormous numbers and were eager as well as trained for battle. The bravery displayed by black soldiers was indicative of their performance throughout the war. Therefore, it is recommended that park officials not only incorporate the achievements of black personnel in their capacities as soldiers and laborers but that personnel are trained to present details concerning the black presence in greater Petersburg."[6]

In many ways the report reveals the consequences of the overall history of public memory of the Crater as well as white Southern control of the battle site. The absence of black interpreters and guides, an interpretation that failed to do justice to salient aspects of the battle and campaign, the lack of relevant literature that could be purchased by visitors, all point to just how deeply embedded the traditional account was within the PNB's institutional structure. The significance of this particular visit by local black students can be found not only in the content of the final report but in the important role that black institutions might continue to play in bringing about changes to the way public historians interpret the battle.[7]

The report's suggestion that the PNB supplement its library and visitors' center with books of broader history pointed to two growing divides, the first between the scholarly pursuits of academic historians and the general public, and the second between the increasing interest among African Americans in seeing their story told at public sites and the preferences of most white Americans, who remained preoccupied with a more traditional battlefield narrative. The problem persisted, however, that few black Americans traveled to Petersburg to visit the Crater, and there was very little indication that this would change in the near future. Without a diverse group of visitors, there was little pressure to tell the complete story or to provide a wider range of reading materials.[8]

While interest in the black experience in the Civil War among professional scholars continued to grow, resulting in ever more sophisticated scholarly studies, it took two events in 1989—the release of the movie *Glory* and Ken Burns's PBS series, *The Civil War*—to introduce the broader public to this relatively unknown aspect of the American past. *Glory* told the story of the men who served in the Fifty-fourth Massachusetts Volunteer Infantry and their commander, Colonel Robert G. Shaw, the account culminating in the failed assault at Battery Wagner in July 1863. The movie, starring Denzel Washington, Morgan Freeman, and Matthew Broderick, offered the general public a heroic account of the trials faced by the men in the regiment and traced the evolution of Shaw's relationship with the men under his command. For many Americans—including Denzel Washington, who won an Academy Award for Best Supporting Actor, and the black actors used as extras in the film—this was their introduction to the history of the Fifty-fourth Massachusetts and the subject of black Civil War soldiers. The film offered its black actors a chance to commemorate and remember the sacrifice of African American soldiers, which in turn led to the organization of a viable black reenacting community and, for a few, a long-term commitment to educating the public. For one reenactor, wearing the blue uniform constituted a tangible "missing link between the Civil War and Civil Rights Movement."[9]

The success of the movie translated into increased attention, once again, to the history of "colored" soldiers in the pages of popular black magazines such as *Jet* and *Ebony*. A lengthy essay featured in the February 1991 issue of *Ebony* included a number of popular colored lithographs depicting black soldiers in battle in places such as Battery Wagner, Petersburg, and Milliken's Bend. The article was preceded by a full-page advertisement: "Pepsi Salutes the Glory of Black History." Echoing the commentary in the movie, the author reminded his readers that after the failed assault at Battery Wagner, these men "provided the margin of difference that turned the tide against the Confederate forces in 1864 and 1865." For black Americans who wished to follow up their visit to the movie theater and explore this history further, *Jet* magazine introduced its readers to Paul Batchelor's extensive collection of war memorabilia and to Don North of Atlanta, who at the time was planning to open a $1.5 million museum devoted to black Civil War soldiers. Despite the popularity of the movie and the critical acclaim it received, some moviegoers viewed the story more as a celebration of Colonel Shaw than as a story about black soldiers. This left some with the lingering question of whether a movie could be made that described the experiences of black soldiers more directly, without having to filter them through the letters and commentary of a white officer.[10]

The movie led to proposals for national monuments to honor African American soldiers. Congresswoman Eleanor Holmes Norton and Washington, D.C., mayor Sharon Pratt Dixon proposed the first national monument in 1991. "When you come to Washington, D.C. and you celebrate the great contributions of Americans," asserted the mayor, "there is one very missing chapter in all of these monuments and all of these expressions." The proposal suggested etching the names of 185,000 black soldiers into granite slabs. Another monument was proposed for a location close to the Vietnam Veterans Memorial on the Washington Mall. These proposals led directly to the dedication of the African American Civil War Memorial in 1998, located in the "U" Street district of the city under the leadership of Frank Smith. The monument includes a wall that lists the names of 209,145 black Union soldiers on 166 burnished stainless steel plaques arranged by regiment. Closer to the Crater, a monument was dedicated to the "valorous service" of USCTs in 1993 at the site of Battery 9, to mark their initial assaults against Petersburg in June 1864. In addition to the dedication of new monuments, Americans also commemorated the 100th anniversary of the dedication of Augustus Saint Gaudens's monument to the Fifty-fourth Massachusetts, located across from the Statehouse on Beacon Street in Boston.[11]

Despite the national public awareness raised by popular Hollywood movies, television programs, and the dedication of new monuments, much of the struggle to broaden interpretation at historic sites throughout the South after the 1960s was carried out most effectively, though not without controversy, by local governments, which had increasingly come to reflect a more interracial and multiethnic citizenry. Political changes throughout the former Confederacy were fueled not only by larger numbers of African Americans going to the polls but also by an emerging self-identification as "Southerners." This identification has led in recent years to large numbers of black Americans moving back to the South.[12]

The Petersburg City Council contained a majority of African Americans by 1973. In 1984, after the resignation of Mayor R. Wilson Cheely, Florence Farley became the first female mayor of Petersburg and the first African American woman to become mayor of a Virginia city. During this same period, the former capital of the Confederacy, Richmond, Virginia, boasted both a black mayor and a predominantly black city council. Such dramatic changes in the racial profile of local government have led to the altering of the city's historical landscape to more accurately reflect its population. Although no sustained attempts were made to remove Richmond's many monuments to its Confederate past during this period, projects that proposed adding monuments to historic sites forced the community to confront tough questions of how the past ought to be remembered and commemorated. This could be seen in the 1995 decision to place a statue of Arthur Ashe on Monument Avenue (within walking distance of statues of "Stonewall" Jackson, Robert E. Lee, J. E. B. Stuart, and Jefferson Davis), and in the April 2003 unveiling of a statue depicting Abraham Lincoln and his son Tad at the Richmond National Battlefield Park, located at the site of the Tredegar Iron Works—a branch of the National Park Service. Challenges to local historic landscapes that reflect competing visions of the past have continued to grow in much of the South over the past ten years.[13]

Changes to historic landscapes in Virginia and other forms of remembrance, especially those associated with the Civil War, evoke strong emotions and contentious debate because they often force the general public to confront the difficult history of slavery and race. The long history of viewing Civil War battlefields as places where brother fought brother and both sides fought for values that were equally honorable continues to be embraced by many. This entrenched view has come under increasing scrutiny from constituencies that wish to connect with historic spaces through an interpretation that more accurately reflects either their family's history or that of their broader community. Failure to change long-standing narratives of the Civil War runs the risk of alienating many. As one visitor to Gettysburg shared, "When you're black, the great battlefield holds mixed messages."[14]

Popular perceptions of the Crater have followed these unstable fault lines. Under the guidance of park historian Chris Calkins, who arrived in 1981, the PNB has made progress both in preserving the physical landscape of Petersburg's battlefields and in expanding the park's interpretation to include coverage of the role of USCTs during the battle as well as to explore broader themes of race and emancipation. In the early 1990s new wayside markers were placed at the Crater site, including one that focuses on Mahone's counterattack and the Confederate reaction to the sight of black soldiers. While there was little debate regarding the decision to use a passage from a well-known letter by William Pegram, in which he conveyed the Confederate outrage over black participation in the Union attack, as part of an audio overview, designers did acknowledge the possibility that some visitors might feel uncomfortable or not approve at all.[15]

Since 2000 the debate over how to interpret Civil War battlefields has been fought in light of the National Park Service's "Rally on the High Ground" symposium, which explored opportunities to broaden its coverage of the battles to include analyses of race and emancipation. The meeting followed on the heels of language added to an appropriations bill by Representative Jesse Jackson Jr., the secretary of the Interior, which directed "the National Park Service managers of Civil War battle sites to recognize and include in all of their public displays and multimedia educational presentations, the unique role that the institution of slavery played in causing the Civil War and its role, if any, at the individual battle sites." Jackson had recently visited twenty Civil War–related sites, and his actions were likely the result of frustration over the absence of black faces. Jackson's own personal conviction that "race . . . is the lens through which I, as an African American, view American history," was also likely meant as a statement made on behalf of the African American community.[16]

The National Park Service held a two-day conference in Ford's The-
atre in Washington, D.C., to discuss ways to meet the goals of the secretary's directive. Professional historians such as James McPherson, Ira
Berlin, Eric Foner, and David Blight dominated the conference, and panels focused on various ways to integrate discussions of the broader concepts
of freedom, democracy, and emancipation into the Park Service's programs. Some in the broader Civil War community continue to view these
changes as reflective of more ominous cultural and political shifts. Southern Heritage groups like the Sons of Confederate Veterans interpret these
changes as reflecting a belief "that the War Between the States was fought
over slavery, period; that therefore all things Confederate are tainted by a
tacit endorsement of slavery or its latter-day counterpart, 'racism,' and
therefore those who venerate them are racists." Others described the decision as an insult to the Confederate soldier, as "South-bashing propagan-
da," or as an "attempt to change the way that a battlefield is interpreted to
include social issues of the day."[17]

Within the National Park Service itself there are lingering disagreements between historians who believe that battlefields are properly interpreted when the focus is on military strategy, tactics, and the experiences
of the soldiers and those who support a more expansive interpretation that
situates the landscape within a social, political, or racial context when
appropriate. It is likely that future historians and frontline interpreters,
trained in the field of public history and introduced to the latest scholarship, will add their voices in favor of an expansive interpretation.[18]

Soon after this reform mandate, the PNB issued a general management plan that addressed every aspect of how it engages visitors: in the
visitors' center, through educational outreach, and especially on the battlefield. The authors of the report acknowledged that new interpretive
themes were necessary, given the past quarter century of scholarship in
cultural, social, and political history. While visitors were already exposed
to the experiences of USCTs during the Petersburg campaign and at the
Crater, an expansive interpretation would go further to show how these
men "took their place as full participants in the army and the Civil War,
although not in society as a whole." This involved explaining the "evolution" and "deployment" of USCTs, demonstrating how the military and
political decisions made in Washington affected black soldiers in Petersburg, and comparing the wartime experiences of these men with postwar
challenges and accomplishments.[19]

Attention to educational outreach by PNB may be the most important step taken to shift and broaden the way the next generation experiences the area's battlefields and other historic resources. Materials include resources for field trips as well as classroom activities. The emphasis on grades 4–6 acknowledges a crucial phase in the cognitive development of children in this age group, as they begin to develop a sense of themselves as part of a larger community that extends into the past. Students can experience life at the Eppes Plantation at City Point by exploring the "experiences of a slave, a plantation owner and a military general through a look at the songs of the period." At the Crater, a park ranger helps students to examine the motivation of Confederate and Union soldiers, including the USCTs: "To have asked Sergeant Decatur Dorsey of the 39th USCT, Private John Haley of the 17th Maine, and Private William Pilcher of the Richmond Artillery Otey Battery, what the cost was that day they might have pointed out the five thousand casualties that changed nothing. Ask them why they fought that day and words like 'freedom,' 'equality,' 'democracy,' and 'home' may have been spoken. Knowing that all three fought until the war's end, you would not have to ask about the depth of commitment." Finally, students can examine copies of Decatur Dorsey's record of service to better understand why he chose to fight and how he experienced life in uniform.[20]

The report also emphasized the importance of forging stronger ties with the surrounding community. The challenges associated with attracting African Americans to Civil War battlefields have deep roots, stemming back to a postwar ambivalence concerning the remembrance and commemoration of a collective past steeped in slavery. Feelings rooted in "shame" and "fear" as well as a lingering suspicion that Civil War battlefields exist to allow the white community to assert the primacy of its experience in that event have proven to be further obstacles to attracting African American visitors. Arguably, no factor in the continued resistance of African Americans to take part in battlefield events is more prominent than the presence of that divisive symbol, the Confederate flag. It is likely that black communities will resist embracing historic sites and other public displays and ceremonies that include what many perceive to be a symbol of "Massive Resistance" and white supremacy.[21]

The park's decision to expand its focus to address the lives of both enslaved and free blacks in the Petersburg area, made to address history important in its own right, was also intended to serve as a bridge to a

Emmanuel Dabney represents a new generation of National Park Service rangers, trained in the latest scholarship and committed to imparting a rich interpretation of the battle that includes issues of race and slavery. (*Petersburg Progress-Index,* August 1, 2010)

community that has, at times, expressed suspicion and a belief that the history represented on the battlefield is not their own. Invited responses from private citizens and local officials to a National Park Service draft proposal suggest that the local community is receptive to these interpretive revisions as a means to attract new constituents, build stronger ties with the community, and encourage tourism in an area that in recent years has experienced financial challenges. Interestingly, it was the decision by the PNB to establish a presence in downtown Petersburg that received the most approval from black civic leaders rather than a project related to the role of USCTs during the campaign. The response also suggests that the National Park Service's visibility within the African American community of Petersburg may be just as important as the expansion of the overall narrative. One sign of this presence is the addition of walking tours of downtown Petersburg led by PNB rangers which, according to a recent news article, have attracted tourists and residents alike.[22]

It goes without saying that the process of building a relationship with the community will take time. For many African Americans who have grown up in Petersburg, the battlefield is still a foreign country. Before the last few decades, children were rarely taught the local black history that would serve to connect them to the battlefield. Richard Stewart, a lifelong resident of Pocahontas Island who has amassed an impressive collection of documents and artifacts related to local history on display in his home, remembers the Crater as the place "where the war was fought" and where an explosion took place. The feeling that there was "nothing" at the Crater "to give meaning to my life" was reinforced during the era of segregation by an unstated belief that the battlefield was the domain of whites. For former Petersburg mayor Rosalyn Dance, the Crater "was a name, but it meant nothing."[23]

The National Park Service staff in Petersburg would have a much more difficult challenge without a working relationship with the local government. In 1994 the city council adopted a plan from the Department of Planning and Community Development that acknowledged, "The events, persons, places, and values of particular importance to African Americans in Petersburg have not been adequately represented." One important observation contained in the report underscores the belief among some local residents that the preservation of African American history ought not to be reduced or understood simply as the preservation of artifacts and historic landscapes. This is especially true for those black residents who are descended from slaves rather than from the vibrant free black population that existed in the city before the Civil War. The uncovering and preservation of ancestral ties between people may be just as important, if not more so, to the former. "Any attempt to gain their widespread involvement," the report concludes, "must include the identification and recording of genealogical connections."[24]

The strong African American presence in local government over the past two decades has created a visible public space for residents to advocate for historic preservation and research that strengthens their identity as members of a community with a rich collective past. In recent years it was discovered that Blandford Cemetery, which contains the graves of the most prominent past members of the community, as well as the beautiful Tiffany windows in Blandford Church commemorating the Confederate cause, also contains the graves of African Americans. Visitors can now look up the names of these individuals in the cemetery's catalogue located in the visitors' center, while the Petersburg Siege Museum now displays artifacts from local black history as part of its permanent exhibit.[25]

Two recent popular depictions of the Crater suggest both continuity and change in our public memory of the battle. The 2003 film *Cold Mountain* opens with a graphic sequence of the battle of the Crater, used to highlight the disillusion of the main character, Inman, with the Confederate war effort. This scene reflects the gap that still exists between narratives that highlight strictly military themes and more recent developments that point to the battle's racial import. The intensity of the explosion is captured, as are the confused reactions of Confederates caught in the middle. The subsequent Union assaults break down, as most of the attacking force gets caught in the crater, which is inaccurately depicted as both too large and much too steep. Still, the close hand-to-hand fighting realistically shows, as few Civil War movies have done in the past, the horror of battle and the relative ease with which Confederates withstood the Union attack.[26]

Any analysis of the movie's depiction of black Union soldiers must keep in mind that the story does not revolve around these men. That said, the production staff made a conscious choice to re-create the battle of the Crater and went to certain lengths to account for some of its salient features. While the battle scenes show glimpses of USCTs as part of the attacking force, it would be impossible for an uneducated viewer to know that they constituted an entire division. Whether minimizing the presence of black soldiers was a conscious choice made during the editing stages or not is impossible to determine; however, at least one scene that did not make the final cut raises the possibility that producers were concerned about how well the racial theme of the battle would be received by the audience. The scene, which takes place after the battle, involves a disgruntled Confederate soldier who notices a severely wounded black soldier crawling on the ground. The Confederate attempts to shoot him but cannot find a loaded weapon, all the while mumbling racial epithets at the wounded man. Finally, after three attempts, the black soldier is executed at point-blank range. Given the difficulty involving the accurate representation of USCTs in the types of interpretations discussed in these pages, it is reasonable to conclude that this scene was cut out of concern that it might alienate or even offend the audience.

Also in 2003 the popular Civil War artist Don Troiani released *Mahone's Counterattack,* which focuses on the attack of the Sixth Virginia and provides a sharp contrast to John Elder's earlier representation of the same moment during the battle. In that earlier painting Elder concentrated on the men of the Twelfth Virginia, while black Union soldiers were shown simply as the objects of Confederate rage. Troiani's depiction of the same event provides an interpretation that falls in line with recent trends in the historiography of USCTs as well as with the desire among many to see these men portrayed as courageous. The men are shown huddled together in the trenches with their white comrades; some are standing to face the Confederate charge while others are fleeing to the rear. Black and white soldiers reflect the full range of emotion and action on the battlefield. Although the title of the painting references Mahone's men, a black soldier stands courageously clutching the Stars and Stripes as a Confederate soldier takes aim in his direction. In today's Civil War art market, Don Troiani's work prominently featuring black Union soldiers as full historical actors is worth acknowledging in contrast to the overwhelming number of prints depicting scenes of the Lost Cause that are bought by consumers who are attracted to those themes. Troiani's painting and *Cold Mountain* suggest that while our understanding of the battle and the role of black soldiers has progressed, there still remains significant unwillingness on the part of the general public to acknowledge the tough issues of race in popular perceptions of Civil War history.

The legacy of reunion and reconciliation that took hold by the turn of the twentieth century and the more recent changes stemming from the cultural and political shifts ensuing from the civil rights movement are likely to continue to reinforce competing memories of the Crater and the Civil War. In contrast to the Civil War centennial, we are likely to see a very different emphasis throughout the Civil War sesquicentennial. The election of Barack Obama in 2008 allowed Americans, both black and white, to peer into the rich and, at times, dark history of race relations to better understand and celebrate this important milestone. Not surprisingly, Obama's election has opened up opportunities to highlight the contributions of African Americans to the Civil War.

In 2009 President Obama was petitioned to discontinue a White House tradition of sending a wreath to the Confederate memorial at Arlington National Cemetery on Memorial Day. Organizers of the petition argued that the monument was "intended as a symbol of white nationalism, portrayed in opposition to the multiracial democracy of Reconstruction, and a celebration of the re-establishment of white supremacy in the

Mahone's Counterattack, Don Troiani's depiction of the Crater, reflects a less heroic depiction of war as well as a richer understanding of the sacrifices made by African Americans. (Historical Art Prints)

former slave states by former Confederate soldiers." The petition received a fair amount of attention in the mainstream media, but Obama, rather than risk the negative fallout from discontinuing a tradition that most Americans were unaware of, chose to maintain the practice but to send a second wreath to the African American Civil War Memorial in Washington, D.C. The decision highlighted the museum, the panels listing the names of USCTs by regiment, and the beautiful monument *The Spirit of Freedom* by sculptor Ed Hamilton.[27]

In contrast, on April 6, 2010, Virginia governor Robert F. McDonnell reinstated Confederate History Month with a proclamation that emphasized the importance of honoring the "the sacrifices of the Confederate leaders, solders and citizens" without a single reference to slavery. The release of the proclamation created a media firestorm. The response to the governor's proclamation reflects the extent to which white and black Americans no longer identify with a Civil War remembrance that fails to acknowledge the centrality of slavery and emancipation to the war in

Virginia. The governor's prompt apology and release of a revised proclamation that included a clear statement pointing to slavery as the war's defining issue demonstrate the influence of a segment of the general public that was shut out from engaging in public discourse just a few decades ago. Both cases point to deeply held competing memories of the Civil War and the difficulty of coming to terms with the history of slavery and race.[28]

The battle over memory of the Crater constitutes one small part of this broader dialogue and will continue to be shaped by it. Disagreements over how to interpret and remember the racial component of the battle of the Crater point to the extent to which Americans are willing to understand the Civil War's significance as something more than a chivalrous contest between white Northerners and Southerners. This will involve resisting the temptation to ignore controversial and potentially divisive questions of race to create a sanitized narrative that downplays issues in favor of emphasizing shared values. While the tendency to suppress uncomfortable facts about race may help render the story more palatable, this would come at the price of sacrificing salient aspects of the history. More important, it suggests that until we are prepared to confront the tough questions about race in our Civil War history and elsewhere, we will continue to struggle to engage in honest dialogue about race in our society today.

ACKNOWLEDGMENTS

I AM GRATEFUL to a number of people who assisted me throughout the research and writing of this book. This project had its roots in a question that was posed in a summer seminar for history teachers at the University of Virginia led by Gary W. Gallagher and William G. Thomas. My inability to identify William Mahone led to a reading of Nelson Blake's 1935 biography and a number of questions about why he had apparently been forgotten in historical memory. Not until I returned to school to complete a master's degree in history at the University of Richmond in 2003 did I have the opportunity to address my questions in a more systematic manner. Thanks to Professor Robert Kenzer for encouraging me to explore Mahone's legacy—along with the battle that he is so closely identified with—as a thesis topic. His timely and thorough comments on multiple drafts were of immense value as I worked to refine my argument. More important, his encouragement to present my work at academic conferences and submit sections of the thesis to journal editors put me in touch with a whole new community that I continue to embrace.

In 2007 Peter Carmichael invited me to submit the manuscript for inclusion in the University Press of Kentucky's New Directions in Southern History series. The process took much longer than I anticipated owing to my responsibilities as a high school history teacher. I especially appreciate Peter's patience and encouragement throughout this period. He never lost interest in the project and understood that my first priority was to my students.

This book would not have been possible without the financial support of the St. Anne's-Belfield School in Charlottesville, Virginia, where I worked for ten years. Thanks to George Conway, former headmaster, and Diana Smith, former dean of academics, for encouraging me to further my education and for making available the school's professional development funds to pay for it. During my tenure at the school I benefited from working with an incredibly talented and passionate faculty. Thanks to Paul Evans, who read an early draft of chapter 3, and to John Noffsinger, who painstakingly read the entire manuscript and offered detailed comments and suggestions to help improve the narrative. Finally, I want to thank my students, who challenged me to be a better teacher, adviser, and historian.

In the summer of 2004, Earl J. Hess contacted me to see if I might be interested in collecting archival material for his planned study of Petersburg's earthworks as well as what became a fine study of the battle of the Crater. Much of the material I collected in Richmond made its way into this book, and I also appreciate Professor Hess's willingness to share material that he had already collected. More recently, Professor Hess provided me with copies of two images from *Battles and Leaders of the Civil War* for this project.

No one has taught me more about the challenges of interpreting the Civil War at our national parks than John Hennessy, chief historian at Fredericksburg & Spotsylvania National Military Park. Our many conversations and battlefield walks remain among the most pleasant and enjoyable experiences of this journey. At the Petersburg National Battlefield, I benefited from Chris Calkins's and James Blankenship's knowledge of the battle and campaign. I also enjoyed spending time with park ranger Emmanuel Dabney, who represents a new generation of National Park Service historians committed to an expansive interpretation of Civil War battlefields that does not ignore the tough questions of race and slavery.

I also benefited from the advice and generosity of a number of scholars, including William Blair, Keith Bohannon, Michael C. Cavanaugh, John Coski, William Freehling, A. Wilson Greene, Mark Grimsley, Caroline E. Janney, Nelson Lankford, William Marvel, Mike Musick, Kenneth W. Noe, Donald R. Shaffer, Aaron Sheehan-Dean, Brooks Simpson, Mark Snell, and Peter Wallenstein. Thanks as well to the research staffs in the Special Collections departments at Duke University, Emory University, the Library of Virginia, the Museum of the Confederacy, the University of Virginia, and the Virginia Historical Society. I want to thank Anne Dean Watkins and the rest of the staff at the University Press of Kentucky for easing this first-time author through the various stages of publication. It has been a pleasure working with them.

A good deal of the material contained in this book was first introduced on my Weblog, *Civil War Memory*, which I began in November 2005. The site has given me the opportunity to test new ideas with a core group of loyal readers who bring a wealth of knowledge and perspective to my work. Rarely did a day go by that I did not receive a blog comment or private e-mail that included sound criticism or pointed me in the direction of new sources. My readers not only helped to further my understanding of the Crater, they enriched my understanding of some of the central issues surrounding how Americans have chosen to remember the Civil War. There are too many people to thank by name and the vast majority I have never met in person, but I hope they will embrace this book as a token of my gratitude.

I owe more to my parents than they will ever know. Their unconditional love and support through some very difficult times provided the foundation for any accomplishments that I can claim. Finally, this book is lovingly dedicated to my wife, Michaela, who has been by my side for the past thirteen years. Ever since visiting the Crater with me for the first time and remarking, "Is that really it?" she has embraced this project with the love and support that continues to bring great joy to my life.

NOTES

Abbreviations

DU	Duke University
EU	Emory University
GDAH	Georgia Department of Archives and History
HSSC	Historical Society of Schuylkill County
LV	Library of Virginia
MC	Museum of the Confederacy
PNB	Petersburg National Battlefield Park
SCL	South Caroliniana Library
UNCC	University of North Carolina at Charlotte
UVA	University of Virginia
VHS	Virginia Historical Society

Introduction

1. Wilson, *Baptized in Blood;* Foster, *Ghosts of the Confederacy;* Brundage, *The Southern Past;* Goldfield, *Still Fighting the Civil War.* A survey of this literature can be found in Brown, "Civil War Remembrance as Reconstruction."

2. Blight, *Race and Reunion.*

3. Blair, *Cities of the Dead.*

4. John Neff also explores the limits of reconciliation in *Honoring the Civil War Dead.*

5. On the role of reunion in the formation of early National Military Parks, see Smith, *This Great Battlefield of Shiloh;* Smith, *The Golden Age of Battlefield Preservation;* Waldrep, *Vicksburg's Long Shadow.* Historians who have examined Civil War memory through battlefield case studies include Reardon, *Pickett's Charge in History and Memory;* Desjardin, *These Honored Dead;* Zenzen, *Battling for Manassas;* Kaser, *At the Bivouac of Memory;* Cimprich, *Fort Pillow.*

6. A growing literature about the way African Americans continued to re-member and commemorate the Civil War has emerged in recent years. See Clark, *Defining Moments;* Fabre and O'Meally, *History and Memory in African-American Culture;* Brundage, *Where These Memories Grow;* Brundage, *The Southern Past* (see chapters 2, 4, and 6).

1. The Battle

1. Bowley, "The Petersburg Mine," 16; Greene, *Civil War Petersburg,* 207–10.

2. A thorough analysis of racism within the Union army and USCT regi-ments specifically can be found in Glatthaar, *Forged in Battle.*

3. Greene, *Civil War Petersburg,* 210.

4. Figures are from Grimsley, *And Keep Moving On,* 224–26.

5. For an overview of the initial stages of the Petersburg campaign, see Cullen, "The Siege of Petersburg"; Eicher, *The Longest Night;* Wert, *The Sword of Lincoln,* 368–75.

6. The most exhaustive account of earthworks in the area around Peters-burg can be found in Hess, *In the Trenches at Petersburg.*

7. Cavanaugh and Marvel, *The Battle of the Crater,* 3–13; on Burnside's role in the construction of the mine and subsequent attack, see Marvel, *Burn-side,* 390–416. Hess, *In the Trenches at Petersburg,* 42.

8. Measurements of the mine can be found in Cavanaugh and Marvel, *The Battle of the Crater,* 11–12. Henry Pleasants to Uncle Henry Pleasants, July 23, 1864, HSSC.

9. On the details of Burnside's initial plan of attack, see Slotkin, *No Quar-ter,* 131–34.

10. Historians have written extensively about the changing attitudes of Union soldiers on issues of race, emancipation, and the recruitment of African American soldiers. Mitchell, *Civil War Soldiers;* McPherson, *For Cause and Comrades;* Manning, *What This Cruel War Was Over.*

11. Trudeau, "A Stranger in the Club."

12. Historians have emphasized the training that the soldiers of the Fourth Division received prior to battle; however, there is scant evidence that this train-ing placed them in a unique position to secure the tactical objectives on the day of battle. Rather, their training functioned more as a refresher course in the manual of arms and various movements that the units would need to execute. See Slotkin, *No Quarter,* 96–102; Hess, *In the Trenches at Petersburg,* 87; Cava-naugh and Marvel, *The Battle of the Crater,* 13–23.

13. Marvel, *Burnside,* 393–95; on James Ledlie, see McWhiney and Jenkins, "The Union's Worst General"; on operations north of the James at Deep Bot-tom, see Suderow, "Glory Denied."

14. Sergeant William Russell, Company H, Twenty-sixth Virginia, Diary, July 30, 1864, PNB; Silliker, *The Rebel Yell and the Yankee Hurrah*, 185; on the physical dimensions of the Crater, see Cullen, "A Report on the Physical History of the Crater," 1975, PNB; Jackson, "Report on Artillery Operations in the Battle of the Crater," 1934, PNB.

15. Shaver, *Gracie's Alabama Brigade*, 68; Stone, *Wandering to Glory*, 189; Power, *Lee's Miserables*, 136.

16. Weld, *War Diary and Letters*, July 30, 1864, 353; Cavanaugh and Marvel, *The Battle of the Crater*, 37–43; Trudeau, *The Last Citadel*, 108–10.

17. Matthew N. Love letter, August 6, 1864, PNB; Letters of Charles J. Mills, HSSC.

18. Cavanaugh and Marvel, *The Battle of the Crater*, 42–53; Trudeau, *Like Men of War*, 236–43; Miller, *The Black Civil War Soldiers of Illinois*, 66–73; on Griffin's attack, see Marvel, "And Fire Shall Devour Them."

19. Cavanaugh and Marvel, *The Battle of the Crater*, 53–88; Trudeau, *The Last Citadel*, 117–18; for a detailed overview of Confederate casualties, see Suderow, "Confederate Casualties at the Crater."

20. Bowley, "The Petersburg Mine," 35. On Mahone's counterattack, see Slotkin, *No Quarter*, 249–70.

21. Whitman, *Civil War Letters*, 127; Trudeau, *The Last Citadel*, 118–27; Cavanaugh and Marvel, *The Battle of the Crater*, 87–103.

22. Casualty figures taken from Slotkin, *No Quarter*, 318; and Hess, *In the Trenches at Petersburg*, 104.

23. Holt, *A Mississippi Rebel in the Army of Northern Virginia*, 288; Bartlett, *Memoir*, 119; Silliker, *The Rebel Yell and the Yankee Hurrah*, 187.

24. Matthew N. Love to his mother, August 6, 1864, PNB; Dorsey Binion to his sister, August 10, 1864, HSSC.

25. Hamilton R. Dunlap Diary, August 1, 1864, HSSC; Henry Family Letters, July 29–August 12, 1864, HSSC.

26. Miller, *The Black Civil War Soldiers of Illinois*, 65.

27. Quoted in Trudeau, "A Stranger in the Club," 113.

28. *Christian Recorder*, June 18, 1864; *Christian Recorder*, November 4, 1865.

29. Quoted in Cornish, *The Sable Arm*, 27; *Christian Recorder*, August 6, 1864; *Baltimore Sun*, August 2, 1864; *Daily Evening Bulletin*, August 1, 1864; *Harper's Weekly*, August 20, 1864.

30. Accounts from Cornish, *The Sable Arm*, 277–78.

31. Cleveland Fisher letter, August 8, 1864, HSSC; Silliker, *The Rebel Yell and the Yankee Hurrah*, 193.

32. Alonzo Rich letter, July 31, 1864, PNB; Charles J. Mills to his mother, July 31, 1864, Letters of Charles J. Mills, HSSC; Edward L. Cook letter, August 4, 1864, HSSC.

33. Edward K. Whitman letter, August 1, 1864, EU; letter from a Union soldier, August 6, 1864, Navarro College; Edward L. Cook letter, August 4, 1864; Kilmer, "The Dash into the Crater," 775–76. See McPherson, *For Cause and Comrades,* 117–30.

34. John F. Sale to his aunt, August 24, 1864, John F. Sale Letters, LV.

35. Rugemer, *The Problem of Emancipation,* 57–91.

36. Ibid., 108–24; Oates, *The First of Jubilee,* 129–45.

37. Hadden, *Slave Patrols,* 167–96.

38. Thomas A. Smith to his sister, August 4, 1864, Thomas A. Smith Letters, UVA; Stevens, *Captain Bill,* 58; Holt, *A Mississippi Rebel in the Army of Northern Virginia,* 287.

39. Laban Odom to his wife, August 2, 1864, Laban Odom Letters, Microfilm Library, GDAH; James Paul Verdery to sister, July 31, 1864, Eugene and James Paul Verdery Papers, DU.

40. Matthew N. Love to his mother, August 6, 1864, PNB; Dorsey Binion to his sister, August 10, 1864, HSSC; William Pegram to his wife, August 1, 1864, in Carroll, *War Letters,* 99.

41. Lee Barfield, "Confederate Letters Written by Mr. Lee Barfield of Dooly County, Georgia, 1861–1865," GDAH; A.T. Fleming to Mrs. N. J. R. Fleming, August 3, 1864, HSSC; Edmund Lockett Womack to Sallie, July 31, 1864, HSSC.

42. For a thorough analysis of the scale of the massacre of USCTs, see Suderow, "The Battle of the Crater." Jerome B. Yates to his wife, August 3, 1864, in Evans, *The 16th Mississippi Infantry,* 281; Henry Van Lewvenigh Bird account, cited in Suderow, "The Battle of the Crater," 223; James Paul Verdery to sister, July 31, 1864, Eugene and James Paul Verdery Papers, DU. William Mahone's Virginia brigade may have understood the danger that armed blacks represented even more than the men of other units that participated in the battle. The five regiments that comprised the Virginia brigade all hailed from areas in the immediate vicinity, including Richmond, Norfolk, Suffolk, and Portsmouth. The Sixty-first Virginia was raised in Petersburg in October 1862. Both the Petersburg Grays and the Petersburg City Guard—both of which joined the Twelfth Virginia Infantry—were part of the security detail at the hanging of John Brown in Charles Town, Virginia, on December 2, 1859. Mahone himself was born and raised in Monroe in Southampton County where Turner's Rebellion took place.

43. Rugemer, *The Problem of Emancipation,* 56; Oates, *The First of Jubilee,* 126.

44. John C. C. Sanders to Pa, August 3, 1864, J. Bailey Thompson Collection, Special Collections, University of Alabama; J. Edward Peterson to sister, August 1, 1864, J. Edward Peterson Papers, Moravian Music Foundation, Winston-Salem, N.C.

45. Alexander, *Fighting for the Confederacy,* 462; Pegram letter, in Carroll,

War Letters, 100; Carmichael, *Lee's Young Artillerist,* 13; Paul M. Higginbotham to his brother, August 1, 1864, VHS.

46. *Petersburg Daily Express,* August 1, 1864.

47. *Richmond Dispatch,* August 2, 1864.

48. *Richmond Examiner,* August 2, 1864.

2. The Lost Cause

1. Henderson, *Petersburg in the Civil War,* 135; Levine, *Confederate Emancipation.*

2. Greene, *Civil War Petersburg,* 260–72.

3. Weeks, *Gettysburg,* 13–35.

4. Robertson, "English Views of the Civil War."

5. Wallace, *History of Petersburg National Battlefield,* 20.

6. *A Guide to the Fortifications and Battlefields around Petersburg.* On tourism in the South during the postwar period, see Silber, *The Romance of Reunion,* 66–92; Wallace, *History of Petersburg National Battlefield,* 19.

7. Trowbridge, *The Desolate South,* 115; Carter, *Magnolia Journey,* 20; Chamberlain, *The Grand Old Man of Maine,* 109.

8. W., letter, 1870, VHS.

9. William Griffith died in 1873, at which time control of the estate fell to his son Timothy, who was only twelve years old at the time of the battle. The young Griffith maintained the site along the lines set by his father, but worked to expand the number and variety of artifacts for display in the museum's "relic house." A collection of the museum's relics, including two bullets that met point to point, was featured in the Century Company's popular four-volume *Battles and Leaders of the Civil War,* published in 1888. Susie Griffith rented the battlefield out for the 1903 reunion and reenactment of the battle and reported a "very large crowd present." The battlefield continued to generate revenue under the auspices of the Griffith family until 1925, when it was sold to the Crater Battlefield Association. Wallace, *History of Petersburg National Battlefield;* Susie R. Griffith to Mrs. M. A. Stephenson, November 10, 1903, Susie R. Griffith Papers, VHS.

10. Pollard, *The Lost Cause,* 537; Pollard, *Southern History of the War,* 197.

11. "The Battle of the Crater"; Happel, "John A. Elder."

12. Hahn, *A Nation under Our Feet,* 206–15; Blair, *Cities of the Dead,* 23–49.

13. "Elder Picture—Virginia Artist," *Richmond Dispatch,* September 28, 1869.

14. "The Battle of the Crater," 98. Mahone purchased the painting for display in his Petersburg home. The painting is currently on display at the Commonwealth Club in Richmond, Virginia.

15. Blair, *Cities of the Dead,* 106–15.

16. Ibid., 119.

17. Linderman, *Embattled Courage*, 266–97. It should be noted that Linderman's study focuses on Union veterans. For an interesting analysis of the continuing ties of esprit de corps in a Union regiment after the war, see Dunkelman, *Brothers One and All*, 251–77.

18. *Petersburg Daily Index-Appeal*, May 11, 1875.

19. "Second Re-union of Mahone's Brigade Held on the Anniversary of the Battle of the Crater," box 2, MC.

20. Ibid.; Foster, *Ghosts of the Confederacy*, 40.

21. "Second Re-union of Mahone's Brigade."

22. McCabe, "Defense of Petersburg," 289.

23. Stewart, *Description of the Battle of the Crater*, 14.

24. On Mahone's life, see Blake, *William Mahone of Virginia*.

25. On Mahone's military career, see ibid., 38–69.

26. See ibid., 79–85; *Petersburg Daily Times*, November 19, 1869, clipping in scrapbook 1, William Mahone Papers, DU.

27. Abram Fulkerson to William Mahone, February 19, 1869, Papers of McGill-Mahone Families, UVA. In addition to consolidation, Mahone also championed plans to bring immigrants to Virginia to further economic development and participated in a convention calling for direct trade with Europe. Clipping in scrapbook 1, William Mahone Papers, DU.

28. "The Battle of the Crater," 98–102; Stephen May, "Flawed Look at How Artists Painted the Conflict," *Washington Times*, September 19, 1998, B2; see letter from John Elder to William Mahone, February 13, 1869, Papers of McGill-Mahone Families, UVA. F. H. Smith to William Mahone, August 11, 1868, Papers of McGill-Mahone Families, UVA; Blake, *William Mahone of Virginia*, 59; John C. Brown to William Mahone, September 14, 1871, correspondence, box 3, William Mahone Papers, DU; see "Charter of the Confederate Burial and Memorial Association," subject files, box 205, William Mahone Papers, DU.

29. R. A. Richardson to William Mahone, June 24, 1868, Papers of McGill-Mahone Families, UVA.

30. De Peyster, "A Military Memoir of William Mahone," 26.

31. Ibid., 31.

32. Newspaper clippings are from the Mahone Scrapbook, Mahone Family Papers, LV; James B. Hope to William Mahone, April 13, 1875, Papers of McGill-Mahone Families, UVA. An account of the involvement of veterans from the Sixty-first Virginia Infantry can be found in Trask, *61st Virginia Infantry*, 34–36.

33. "Second Re-union of Mahone's Brigade."

34. See the letter from James B. Hope to William Mahone, April 17, 1875, Papers of McGill-Mahone Families, UVA; in addition, see correspondence in boxes 4, 8, and 11, William Mahone Papers, DU. Mahone's close supporters in-

cluded Joseph Minnitree; V. D. Gromer, who would be Mahone's choice for lieutenant governor in 1881; the future Readjuster governor William E. Cameron; and James B. Hope, who was editor of the *Norfolk Landmark*.

3. Virginia's Reconstruction

1. Robert W. Bagby, "Gen. Mahone and the Third Georgia Re-union," *Enterprise,* July 27, 1883, clipping in scrapbook folder 4, Mahone Family Papers, 1866–1900, LV.

2. At least six Virginia politicians and editors engaged in duels in this period (Moore, "The Death of the Duel"). For a thorough overview of Lost Cause ideology, see Alan T. Nolan, "The Anatomy of the Myth," in Gallagher and Nolan, *The Myth of the Lost Cause,* 11–34. The most thorough treatment of the Lost Cause movement can be found in Foster, *Ghosts of the Confederacy;* Pressly, *Americans Interpret Their Civil War,* 101–26. On James Longstreet's postwar career, see Piston, *Lee's Tarnished Lieutenant,* 129–36; Wert, *General James Longstreet,* 407–27.

3. For two recent studies that examine conditions in the postwar South that shaped early histories of the war, see Blight, *Race and Reunion,* especially 293 for a brief reference to the influence of Mahone and the Readjusters on Lost Cause ideology, and Goldfield, *Still Fighting the Civil War.*

4. On Mahone, the state debt, and the Readjusters, see Dailey, *Before Jim Crow;* Hahn, *A Nation under Our Feet,* 367–93; Moore, *Two Paths to the New South;* Degler, *Other South,* 270–315. Quote from Degler, *Other South,* 276–78.

5. On the history of the funding debate and regional alignments, see Blake, *William Mahone of Virginia,* 156–95; Dailey, *Before Jim Crow,* 15–47; Degler, *Other South,* 280–81.

6. Bagby, *John Brown and William Mahone,* 5.

7. "General Mahone Can't Understand the Times," clipping in Harrison Southworth Scrapbook, UVA.

8. "The Soldier and the Debt," 1880, clipping in scrapbook 1, William Mahone Papers, DU; "Sympathizing with Mahone," *New York Herald,* September 6, 1880, reprinted from *Southern Intelligencer,* clipping in scrapbook 1, William Mahone Papers, DU.

9. *Richmond State,* September 1, 1880, clipping in scrapbook 13, box 210, DU; "Mahone as a Soldier," *Troy Messenger,* April 1881, clipping in scrapbook 19, box 212, DU; *Iowa Intelligencer,* March 24, 1881, clipping in scrapbook 19, box 212, DU; *Landmark,* March 2, 1881, clipping in scrapbook 5, box 207, DU.

10. "Mahone's Private Life," *Capital,* May 22, 1881, clipping in scrapbook 19, box 212, DU; *Wedge,* May 1882, clipping in scrapbook 28, box 215, DU.

11. Blake, *William Mahone of Virginia,* 199–212.

12. Degler, *Other South,* 282–85; Blake, *William Mahone of Virginia,* 182–95;

Lawrence L. Hartzell, "The Exploration of Freedom in Black Petersburg, Virginia, 1865–1902," in Ayers and Willis, *The Edge of the South,* 140–43.

13. Statistics can be found in Dailey, *Before Jim Crow,* 67; Alexander, *Race Man,* 21.

14. Williams, *A Sketch of the Life and Times of Capt. R. A. Paul,* 16–17.

15. "Past and Present," *National Republican,* April 22, 1881, clipping in scrapbook 19, box 212, DU; "The People of Virginia Must Save Virginia," *Richmond State,* September 12, 1881, DU.

16. *A Correspondence between Generals Early and Mahone, in Regards to the Military Memoir of the Latter,* 1881, 3, DU.

17. "Longstreet, Mosby, and Now Mahone," *Charleston Mercury,* reprinted from *New York Herald,* clipping in scrapbook 19, box 212, DU; "A Mahone Movement in Georgia," *Constitution,* December 14, 1881, clipping in scrapbook 28, box 215, DU. On the spread of independent movements throughout the South, see Degler, *Other South,* 288–91.

18. *Petersburg Index-Appeal,* December 6, 1881. On Virginia's legislative program to aid disabled Confederates, see Dickens, "An Arm and a Leg for the Confederacy"; *Mahoneism Unveiled!*

19. "A Soldier from Bethel to Appomattox," *Richmond Whig,* May 30, 1872, clipping in scrapbook 29, box 215, DU; "William Mahone: One of His Old Brigade Speaks," *National Republican,* August 1882, clipping in scrapbook 29, box 215, DU.

20. See Levin, "'On That Day,'" 27–28.

21. Quoted in Bernard, *War Talks of Confederate Veterans,* 216–18.

22. "The Crater!" *Richmond Commonwealth,* August 21, 1880, clipping in William Mahone Scrapbook, Mahone Family Papers, LV. As a point of comparison, Carol Reardon concluded that Virginia's veterans of Longstreet's Corps maintained their allegiance throughout the postwar years ("James Longstreet's Virginia Defenders," in Gallagher, *Three Days at Gettysburg,* 245–69).

23. "The Crater!" Although it easy to view Weisiger's account as politically motivated, his own understanding of the battle had changed little since April 1872, when Mahone requested an account to aid in his ongoing debate with Cadmus Wilcox and the fallout surrounding the De Peyster sketch. Weisiger claimed that he had received orders to wait for the command to charge but noticed Union soldiers forming for an attack and deemed it necessary to proceed on his own. Weisiger made no mention of having interacted with Mahone once through the covered way and poised for the attack. Given the confusion both in and around the crater, it is possible that Weisiger did not see Mahone taking steps to organize an attack. More important, there is no record of Mahone having responded to Weisiger's letter (David Weisiger to William Mahone, April 25, 1872, correspondence, box 4, March–April 1872, William Mahone Papers, DU).

24. Clipping in William Mahone Scrapbook, Mahone Family Papers, LV.

25. "Gen. Mahone and the Crater," Harrison Southworth Scrapbook, UVA.

26. On the Danville riot, see Dailey, *Before Jim Crow,* 119–25; Degler, *Other South,* 292–300.

27. Clippings in Harrison Southworth Scrapbook, UVA.

28. "Gen. Lee in Rockbridge," clipping in scrapbook 32, box 216; "The Gallant Fitz in Buckingham Courthouse," clipping in scrapbook 32, box 216, both in William Mahone Papers, DU.

29. Blake, *William Mahone of Virginia,* 234–54.

30. Noe, "'Damned North Carolinians' and 'Brave Virginians.'"

31. Lane, "The Truth of History"; Noe, "'Damned North Carolinians' and 'Brave Virginians,'" 1111.

32. *Norfolk Landmark,* October 9, 1895; *Portsmouth Star,* October 9, 1865.

4. Reinforcing the Status Quo

1. Stith Bolling was the first president of the Petersburg National Battlefield Association. During the war he served as a captain in the cavalry and as an assistant adjutant general on the staff of Major General William Henry Fitzhugh Lee. "Cannon Flash and Roar on Historic Crater Battlefield," *Richmond Times-Dispatch,* November 7, 1903.

2. "Cannon Flash and Roar," *Richmond Times-Dispatch,* November 7, 1903; "The Battle of the Crater," *Petersburg Daily Index-Appeal,* November 7, 1903.

3. "Cannon Flash and Roar."

4. Foster, *Ghosts of the Confederacy,* 140; Smith, *Managing White Supremacy,* 29.

5. "Cannon Flash and Roar"; "The Battle of the Crater."

6. Rogers, "The Crater Battle," 14; Wise, *The End of an Era,* 11–12.

7. Smith, *Managing White Supremacy,* 20, 26–28. See also Wallenstein, *Blue Laws and Black Codes,* 1–9; Dailey, *Before Jim Crow,* 161–69.

8. William H. Stewart, ed. "The Charge of the Crater: Personal Statements by Participants," MC; Alfred Lewis Scott Memoir, Special Collections, VHS. Scott served in the Ninth Alabama Infantry Regiment.

9. Day, "Battle of the Crater," 356; Vance, "Incidents of the Crater Battle," 178.

10. Dodge, *A Bird's-Eye View of Our Civil War,* 248–51.

11. Glatthaar, *Forged in Battle,* 231–64.

12. Thomas, "The Colored Troops at Petersburg," 777.

13. D. E. Proctor, "The Massacre in the Crater," *National Tribune,* October 17, 1907.

14. Frank Holsinger, "The Colored Troops at the Crater," *National Tribune,* October 19, 1905; J. Q. Adams, "Battle of the Crater," *National Tribune,* June 25, 1903.

15. Delavan Bates, "A Day with the Colored Troops," *National Tribune,* January 30, 1908.

16. On Bowley's view of the war, see the introduction to Watson, *Honor in Command,* 1–41. Quote in ibid., 139.

17. Ibid., 137; on the massacre of USCTs, see 152–56.

18. Henderson, *Gilded Age City,* 121–48.

19. Ibid., 311–26.

20. On Virginia's black militia companies, see Cunningham, "They Are as Proud of Their Uniform as Any Who Serve Virginia."

21. Quoted in Henderson, *Gilded Age City,* 330–31.

22. *Petersburg Lancet* article quoted in Kachun, *Festivals of Freedom,* 149.

23. Cunningham, "They Are as Proud of Their Uniform as Any Who Serve Virginia."

24. Brundage, *The Southern Past,* 138–82.

25. Franklin, *George Washington Williams;* Williams, *A History of the Negro Troops,* xiii–xiv.

26. Williams, *A History of the Negro Troops,* 249–50; Thanks to Peter Luebke for pointing out this likely reason as to why Williams fails to reference the massacre at the Crater.

27. Johnson, *A School History of the Negro Race,* 3–4, 126–28.

28. Shaffer, *After the Glory,* 180–85.

5. Whites Only

1. *New York Times,* November 15, 1903; Foster, *Ghosts of the Confederacy,* 145–49; Traxel, *1898,* 144–53.

2. Captain Fred E. Waldron to Ella Merrit, June 20, 1865, Ella Merrit File, SCL. Waldron's letter went unanswered, and this lack of response prompted another letter, this time written from New York City in late September. It is unknown whether Waldron ever received a response to this second letter.

3. *Petersburg Daily Index-Appeal,* October 15, 1885.

4. *Petersburg Daily Index-Appeal,* May 4, 1887.

5. "To Buy the Crater Farm," *New York Times,* March 1, 1896.

6. Gould, *The Story of the Forty-eighth,* 393; Veterans from the Forty-eighth Pennsylvania reached out to Confederate veterans at least one year before their trip to Petersburg. Captain John C. Featherston, who served in Mahone's Division at the Crater, was invited to Pottsville, Pennsylvania, in April 1906 to deliver an address to help raise funds for their proposed monument.

7. Embick, *Military History of the Third Division,* 70–82.

8. "Famous Fight at the Crater," *New York Times,* July 30, 1895; John S. Wood, "The Famous Crater and Other Landmarks May Soon Disappear," *New York Times,* April 24, 1916.

9. John D. Wells, "The Scars of War: Battlefields of Northern Virginia Forty-five Years After," *Metropolitan,* February 1907, 531–49.

10. Scott and Wyatt, *Petersburg's Story,* 312–12, 340–41.

11. Carter R. Bishop, "The Cockade City of the Union: Petersburg, Virginia," 1907, UVA. Bishop saw little action during the war. Admitted to the Virginia Military Institute in 1864, he was called into service at the beginning of April 1865 but was captured. In 1875 he returned to Petersburg to begin a career as a bank cashier and civil engineer. His rank was honorary.

12. The decline of Petersburg's economy is tracked in Henderson, *Gilded Age City,* 473–79; Scott and Wyatt, *Petersburg's Story,* 288–94.

13. *Petersburg Daily Index-Appeal,* May 3, 1907; speech by Walter A. Watson, Walter A. Watson Papers, VHS.

14. *Petersburg Daily Index-Appeal,* May 3, 1907; *Petersburg Daily Index-Appeal,* May 19, 1907.

15. Wallace, *History of the Petersburg National Battlefield,* 43–50.

16. Ibid., 50–52; George S. Bernard to Gordon McCabe, November 1, 1911, Virginia Miscellaneous Papers (Section 6), VHS.

17. Senator Wadsworth may have been interested due to the fact that his father, Major General James W. Wadsworth, was mortally wounded at the Wilderness, and later a fort constructed by Union forces on the Weldon Railroad in 1864 had been named for him. Wallace, *History of Petersburg National Battlefield,* 56–58; "Park at Old Petersburg," *New York Times,* April 3, 1927.

18. Johnson, *Douglas Southall Freeman,* 54–57; Freeman, *Robert E. Lee;* Freeman, *Lee's Lieutenants.*

19. Johnson, *Douglas Southall Freeman,* 78–80.

20. "Tragic Petersburg Crater Draws Civil War Pilgrims," *New York Times,* August 23, 1925.

21. "Civil War Field for Golf Course," *New York Times,* April 22, 1928.

22. "The 'Crater' and Battlefield Museum," UNCC.

23. On at least two occasions during the association's ownership of the battlefield, the bodies of soldiers were uncovered in the area around the crater. In March 1928, one Union soldier was unearthed and reburied by the A. P. Hill Camp. The flag that draped the casket was sent to the governor of Massachusetts. "Fuller Receives Flags of North and South in Boston Ceremony," *New York Times,* March 6, 1928. Three years later, in March 1931, the bodies of twenty-nine Union soldiers were handed over to the A. P. Hill Camp for reburial. Carter Bishop requested that all Confederate veterans attend the service, which was to take place in Petersburg along with a company from the National Guard. See "To Honor Union Soldiers," *New York Times,* April 9, 1931.

24. Wallace, *History of the Petersburg National Battlefield,* 96–97. Even after the National Park Service purchased the Crater, area residents pushed for the

reopening of the golf course as a municipal project. Support for this project could be found in Petersburg's civic organizations as well as the city council.

25. United States Department of the Interior, National Park Service, Markers for Erection in the Petersburg National Military Park, "Battle of the Crater," Douglas Southall Freeman Papers, box 1, Battlefield Parks, 1934–1937, UVA.

26. Wallace, *History of the Petersburg National Battlefield,* 98–99.

27. *Richmond Times-Dispatch,* April 23, 1937.

28. "Will Re-enact Battle of Crater in Virginia," *New York Times,* April 25, 1937; *Richmond Times-Dispatch,* April 30, 1937.

29. "Battle of the Crater Dialogue," Douglas Southall Freeman Papers, box 5, UVA; "Battle of the Crater," program, author's collection.

30. Wallace, *History of the Petersburg National Battlefield,* 99–100; *Richmond Times-Dispatch,* April 30, 1937; *Petersburg Progress-Index,* August 2, 1937; Harrison, *Home to the Cockade City,* 87.

31. *Richmond Times-Dispatch,* April 29, 1937.

6. Competing Memories

1. On postwar heritage vacations, see chapter 2 in Rugh, *Are We There Yet?*

2. In 1954, the National Park Service recorded 206,864 visitors. Conway, *History of Petersburg National Battlefield,* 118.

3. Ibid., 100–102, 108–11.

4. *Superintendent's Annual Reports,* PNB; Conway, *History of Petersburg National Battlefield,* 118–22. While Mahone's role at the Crater was generally celebrated, he continued to come under fire in reference to his foray into Virginia politics and leadership of the Readjuster Party. As late as the 1940s, critics accused Mahone of disloyalty to his men and to the Commonwealth. See Harrison, *Home to the Cockade City,* 114–17; Moger, *Virginia,* 69.

5. "Interest in Park Dates from 1865," newspaper and date unknown (c. 1956), in PNB files; *Petersburg National Military Park,* 1942, author's collection; Lykes, *Petersburg Battlefields,* 12–22.

6. "Educational Value of Battlefield Park Stressed," *Petersburg Progress-Index,* May 15, 1934; Superintendent's Report (Monthly Narratives): Report on Administrative and Personnel, May 1937, PNB.

7. Conway, *History of Petersburg National Battlefield,* 138–39; Trevvett Matthews, "Battlefield Park Map Is Prized Possession," unknown newspaper, PNB.

8. Conway, *History of Petersburg National Battlefield,* 4–7; Shackel, *Memory in Black and White,* 161.

9. Kammen, *Mystic Chords of Memory,* 593–94.

10. *Report of the Preliminary Plans of the Virginia Civil War Commission to the General Assembly,* 21.

11. *Virginia's Opportunity*, 21.

12. "The Civil War Centennial in Petersburg"; *Virginia's Opportunity*, 10.

13. Jon Wiener, "Civil War, Cold War, Civil Rights: The Civil War Centennial in Context, 1960–1965," in Fahs and Waugh, *The Memory of the Civil War in American Culture*, 237.

14. Cook, *Troubled Commemoration*, 88–113.

15. On the 1961 Manassas reenactment, see Shackel, *Memory in Black and White*, 161–65; Bamberger quoted in Arsenault, *Freedom Riders*, 335.

16. Robert Cook, "Unfinished Business: African Americans and the Civil War Centennial," in Grant and Parish, *Legacy of Disunion*, 57; Randolph quote in Cook, "(Un)Furl That Banner," 897; "The Civil War Centennial and the Negro," 3.

17. Cornish, *The Sable Arm;* Quarles, *The Negro in the Civil War.*

18. "Tan Troops Played Vital Role in Both Armies of Civil War," *Richmond Afro-American*, February 4, 1961; "Colored Troops in Forefront on the Day That Richmond Fell," *Richmond Afro-American*, March 16, 1963.

19. Lerone Bennett Jr., "The Negro in the Civil War," *Ebony*, June 1962, 132–37; "These Truly Are the Brave," *Ebony*, August 1968, 164–77; "Paradox of the Black Soldier" editorial can be found on 142 of the latter issue.

20. Letters to *Ebony* quoted in Cook, *Troubled Commemoration*, 168–69.

21. "Yesterday in Negro History," *Jet*, August 1, 1963, 11; "Seeks Unclaimed Bonuses of Civil War Ancestors," *Jet*, January 23, 1964, 10.

22. Interview with Frank Smith, July 23, 2007, Washington, D.C.

23. Howard N. Meyer, "The Neglected Tool," *Crisis*, November 1963, 529–32.

24. *The Negro History Bulletin*, December 1961, 58; editorial by Benjamin Quarles in *Negro History Bulletin*, December 1960, 50, 52. Examples of textbooks used at this time include Morris Goodman, *A Junior History of the American Negro*, vol. 1 (New York: Fleet, 1969): "The Negro enlisted man was a fine soldier. He went into the service knowing what he was fighting for: to gain self respect, the respect of others, and a new chance for his sons and daughters. The Negro soldiers fought nobly, even though their training and supplies were not as good as those whites received" (115).

25. Editorial in *Freedomways*, Winter 1963, 5; Cook, "Unfinished Business," 61–63.

26. Pritched and Toppin, "The Relationship between Black Voting Power and Desegregation in Petersburg," 2–3.

27. Williams, "The Civil Rights Movement in Richmond and Petersburg," 18–36.

28. Arsenault, *Freedom Riders*, 114–17.

29. "The Event Deserves Attendance," *Petersburg Progress-Index*, July 29, 1964.

30. Stephens, "Participation of Negro Troops in 'the Battle of the Crater,'" 97.

7. Moving Forward

1. "New Historical Markers at Park to Cite Blacks," *Petersburg Progress-Index,* July 9, 1974; "Battlefield Park Named as Site of Black History," *Petersburg Progress-Index,* July 16, 1974; LeeNora Everett, "Petersburg Battlefield Stressing Black Soldier," *Richmond Times-Dispatch,* July 14, 1975. The marker was not formally dedicated until 1988 owing to financial difficulty.

2. For a thorough analysis of post–civil rights historical revisions to public and private historical institutions, see Brundage, *The Southern Past,* 270–315; on Colonial Williamsburg, see Greenspan, *Creating Colonial Williamsburg,* specifically chapters 6 and 7; Joanne Melish, "Recovering (from) Slavery: Four Struggles to Tell the Truth," in Horton and Horton, *Slavery and Public History,* 103–33.

3. Brundage, *The Southern Past,* 295.

4. On the historiography of slavery, see Peter Kolchin, "Slavery and Freedom in the Civil War South," in McPherson and Cooper, *Writing the Civil War,* 241–60; on recent developments in Civil War history, see Joseph T. Glatthaar, "The 'New' Civil War History: An Overview," *Pennsylvania Magazine of History and Biography,* July 1991, 339–69.

5. "Afro-American History Interpretation at Selected National Parks" (report prepared by research team, Department of History, Howard University, 1978), 145, PNB.

6. Ibid., 146, 151.

7. The lack of scholarship related to black history available for purchase was part of a much larger problem concerning the content of history textbooks used in public schools throughout Virginia. In 1948, the Virginia General Assembly, controlled by the Democratic Party, created a textbook commission to impose its own version of history in Virginia public schools. The assembly mandated that students—both black and white—learn the state's history from books authorized and edited by the commission. Changes to these textbooks were made during the 1950s and 1960s and reflected a traditional Lost Cause version of slavery, the Civil War, and Reconstruction. Even by the end of the 1970s students in scattered Virginia counties could be found reading the popular title *Virginia: History, Government, Geography,* by Francis B. Simkins, Spotswood H. Jones, and Sidman P. Poole. Students learned that during the 1850s slaves "were not worried by the furious arguments going on between Northerners and Southerners over what should be done with them. In fact, they paid little attention to these arguments." See Dean, "'Who Controls the Past Controls the Future.'"

8. "Afro-American History Interpretation," 147. For a survey of this literature, see Kolchin, "Slavery and Freedom in the Civil War South." On the historiography of slavery through the 1980s, see Peter J. Parish's bibliographical essay in *Slavery,* 167–88.

9. Interview with Mel Reid, Jerry Brown, and Ben Hawley, July 23, 2007, Washington, D.C. None of the individuals interviewed remembers learning about black Civil War soldiers in primary school, which suggests that historians use caution in assessing the influence of publications from the 1960s in the nation's public schools. The wide gap between professional historians and the general public can be seen in the critical assessments that both movies received following their release. See Leon F. Litwack, "The Historian, the Filmmaker, and the Civil War," in Toplin, *Ken Burns's* The Civil War, 119–40; Martin H. Blatt, "*Glory:* Hollywood History, Popular Culture, and the Fifty-fourth Massachusetts Regiment," in Blatt, Brown, and Yacovone, *Hope and Glory*, 215–35.

10. "Black, Blue, and Gray: The Other Civil War," *Ebony,* February 1991, 98–105; "History Buffs Keep Memory of Civil War Soldiers Alive," *Jet,* March 12, 1990, 32; interview with Frank Smith, July 23, 2007.

11. "Memorial for Black Patriots Announced in Nation's Capital," *Jet,* September 2, 1991, 31; "Ceremony Held for 100th Anniversary of Monument Honoring Famed Black Regiment," *Jet,* June 23, 1997, 20–21.

12. Goldfield, *Still Fighting the Civil War,* 283–89.

13. Marie Tyler-McGraw, "Southern Comfort Levels: Race, Heritage Tourism, and the Civil War in Richmond," in Horton and Horton, *Slavery and Public History,* 151–67; on recent debates about the public display of the Confederate flag, see Coski, *The Confederate Battle Flag,* specifically chapters 9–13.

14. Allen B. Ballard, "The Demons of Gettysburg," *New York Times,* May 30, 1999.

15. Interview with John Hennessy, July 18, 2007, Fredericksburg, Va. In May 2005 the Petersburg National Battlefield cosponsored a two-day conference at Virginia State University on African Americans and the Civil War. Topics focused on a wide range of subjects relating to the African American experience during the Civil War and postwar years.

16. Sutton, *Rally on the High Ground;* "Rep. Jesse Jackson Jr. Wins Move for National Sites to Recognize Slavery's Role in Civil War History," *Jet,* May 29, 2000, 20.

17. For a thorough analysis of the reactions to the National Park Service decision, see Dwight T. Pitcaithley, "'A Cosmic Threat': The National Park Service Addresses the Causes of the American Civil War," in Horton and Horton, *Slavery and Public History,* 169–86.

18. Getz, "Looking to the Higher Ground."

19. *Petersburg National Battlefield: Final General Management Plan,* 39. Much has been made of the significance of the Rally symposium in leading to more recent shifts in interpretation, but it should be noted that many battlefield sites were already in the process of expanding their site interpretations to include subjects related to the African American experience. Interview with John Hennessy, July 18, 2007.

20. *Petersburg National Battlefield: Educator's Guide,* 8–9, 18–19.

21. Interview with Mel Reid, Jerry Brown, and Ben Hawley, July 23, 2007; interview with John Hennessy, July 18, 2007.

22. *Petersburg National Battlefield: Final General Management Plan,* 39–40. Letters of response to the Park Service's proposal can be found on 82–168. F. M. Wiggins, "Retracing the Path of Slavery," *Petersburg Progress-Index,* July 8, 2007. A calendar of events focused on the home front during the war and sponsored by the PNB includes the programs "Life and Work of Petersburg's Enslaved" and "Siege of Petersburg: Let Your Voices Be Heard!" Brochures can also be found in the community with titles such as "African-Americans at Petersburg" and "African Americans on Lee's Retreat, April 1865."

23. Interview with Richard Stewart, July 16, 2007, Petersburg, Va.; interview with Rosalyn Dance, July 16, 2007, Petersburg, Va. Ms. Dance currently serves as a state delegate from Virginia's Sixty-third District.

24. Mary Ellen Bushy, Ann Creighton-Zollar, Lucious Edwards Jr., L. Daniel Mouer, and Robin L. Ryder, "African Americans in Petersburg: Historic Contexts and Resources for Preservation Planning, Research and Interpretation" (report presented to the City of Petersburg, Department of Planning and Community Development, 1994), 1–3.

25. Interview with Rosalyn Dance, July 16, 2007.

26. For analysis of the film's historical themes from Ed Ayers, Gary Gallagher, and Stephen Cushman, see Bob Thompson, "Hollywood as 'History': Big Battle Is Impressive, but Where's Slavery?" *Seattle Times,* December 27, 2003.

27. Edward Sebesta and James Loewen, "Dear President Obama: Please Don't Honor the Arlington Confederate Monument," History News Network, George Mason University, http://hnn.us/articles/85884.html (accessed August 2, 2010). The memorial was developed by the African American Civil War Memorial Freedom Foundation and Museum and was transferred to the National Park Service on October 27, 2004. The National Mall and Memorial Parks of the National Park Service currently manage the site.

28. Gallagher, "Reevaluating Virginia's 'Shared History.'"

BIBLIOGRAPHY

Manuscript and Archival Material

Auburn University, Auburn, Alabama
    Emily S. York Papers
Cornell University Library, Division of Rare Books and Manuscript Collections, Ithaca, New York
    Henry Chamberlain Papers
Duke University Library, Rare Book, Manuscript, and Special Collections Library, Durham, North Carolina
    A Correspondence between Generals Early and Mahone, in Regards to the Military Memoir of the Latter, 1881
    William Mahone Papers
    Eugene and James Paul Verdery Papers
Emory University, Special Collections, Robert W. Woodruff Library, Atlanta, Georgia
    Benjamin Wesley Justice Papers
    Edward K. Whitman Letters
Georgia Department of Archives and History, Atlanta
    Lee Barfield Letters
    Laban Odom Letters
Historical Society of Schuylkill County, Schuylkill County, Pennsylvania
    Samuel Beddall Diary
    Dorsey Binion Letters
    Edward L. Cook letter
    Hamilton R. Dunlap Diary
    Cleveland Fisher letter
    A. T. Fleming Letters
    Henry Family Letters
    Benjamin Mason Letters

Charles J. Mills Letters
Henry Pleasants Letters
Edmund L. Womack Letters
Library of Virginia, Richmond
David F. Dobie Papers
Mahone Family Papers
John F. Sale Letters
Moravian Music Foundation, Winston-Salem, North Carolina
J. Edward Peterson Papers
Museum of the Confederacy, Richmond, Virginia
Anthony S. Barksdale Papers
"Second Re-union of Mahone's Brigade Held on the Anniversary of the
Battle of the Crater"
Stewart, William H., ed. "The Charge of the Crater: Personal Statements
by Participants"
John Winsmith Papers
Navarro College, Corsicana, Texas
William L. Hyde Papers
Union soldier letter, August 6, 1864
North Carolina Department of Archives and History, Raleigh
John M. Lewis Confederate Pension Application File
Petersburg National Battlefield Park, Petersburg, Virginia
"Afro-American History Interpretation at Selected National Parks"
(report prepared by research team, Department of History, Howard
University, 1978)
Charles Campbell Diary
Cullen, Joseph P. "Report on the Physical History of the Crater," 1975
Houts, Joseph K., ed. "A Darkness Ablaze" (manuscript copy)
Jackson, C. R. "Report on Artillery Operations in the Battle of the
Crater," 1934
Matthew N. Love letter, August 6, 1864
Alonzo Rich letter, July 31, 1864
Sergeant William Russell Diary
S. S. Watson Letters
Superintendent's Annual Reports
Superintendent's Report (Monthly Narratives): Report on Administrative
and Personnel, May 1937
South Caroliniana Library, Columbia
Stephen G. Elliott Papers
Ella Merrit File
Moseley Family Papers

University of Alabama, Tuscaloosa
    J. Bailey Thompson Collection
University of North Carolina at Charlotte, Atkins Library
    "The 'Crater' and Battlefield Museum" (brochure)
    Emma Echols Papers
    William L. Faulkner letter
University of Notre Dame, South Bend, Indiana
    John M. Jackson Letters
University of Southern Mississippi, Hattiesburg
    Letters of Hugh Carroll Dickson
University of Virginia, Alderman Library, Charlottesville
    George Bernard Papers
    Bishop, Carter R. "The Cockade City of the Union: Petersburg,
        Virginia," 1907
    John H. Claiborne Letters
    Hugh Thomas Douglas Papers
    Douglas Southall Freeman Papers
    Papers of McGill-Mahone Families
    Thomas A. Smith Letters
    Harrison Southworth Scrapbook
    E. N. Wise Papers
Vermont Historical Society, Barre
    Barton Family Papers
Virginia Historical Society, Richmond
    Ellzey, Mason G. "The Cause We Lost and the Land We Love"
    "General William Mahone, the 'Hero of the Crater'" (broadside)
    Susie R. Griffith Papers
    William H. Harris Journal
    Paul Higginbotham letter
    John Marshall Martin Papers
    Alfred Lewis Scott Memoir
    Virginia Miscellaneous Papers
    W. letter, 1870
    Walter A. Watson Papers
    William Family Papers
Virginia Polytechnic and State University, Blacksburg
    Daniel Blain Letters

Interviews

Brown, Jerry. Personal interview. July 23, 2007.
Dance, Rosalyn. Personal interview. July 23, 2007.

Hawley, Ben. Personal interview. July 23, 2007.
Hennessy, John. Personal interview. July 18, 2007.
Reid, Mel. Personal interview. July 23, 2007.
Smith, Frank. Personal interview. July 23, 2007.
Stewart, Richard. Personal interview. July 16, 2007.

Government Documents

African Americans in Petersburg: Historic Contexts and Resources for Preservation Planning, Research and Interpretation. Petersburg: Department of Planning and Community Development, 1994.

Bushy, Mary Ellen, Ann Creighton-Zollar, Lucious Edwards Jr., L. Daniel Mouer, and Robin L. Ryder, *African Americans in Petersburg: Historic Contexts and Resources for Preservation Planning, Research and Interpretation.* Petersburg: Department of Planning and Community Development, 1994.

The Civil War Centennial in Petersburg. Petersburg: Petersburg Chamber of Commerce, 1961.

Conway, Martin R. *A History of Petersburg National Battlefield: 1857–1982.* Washington, D.C.: Department of the Interior, 1983.

Lykes, Richard W. *Petersburg Battlefields.* National Park Service Handbook Series no. 13. Washington, D.C.: Department of the Interior, 1950.

Report of the Preliminary Plans of the Virginia Civil War Commission to the General Assembly. Richmond: Virginia Civil War Commission, 1959.

U.S. War Department. *The War of the Rebellion: A Compilation of the Official Records of the Union and Confederate Armies.* 128 vols. Washington, D.C.: Government Printing Office, 1880–1901.

Virginia's Opportunity: The Civil War Centennial, 1961–1965. Richmond: Virginia Civil War Commission, 1960.

Wallace, Lee. *A History of Petersburg National Battlefield to 1956.* Washington, D.C.: Department of the Interior, 1983.

Primary Sources

Alexander, Edward Porter. *Fighting for the Confederacy: The Personal Recollections of General Edward Porter Alexander.* Edited by Gary W. Gallagher. Chapel Hill: University of North Carolina Press, 1989.

Anderson, John. *The Fifty-seventh Regiment of Massachusetts Volunteers in the War of Rebellion.* Boston: E. B. Stillings, 1896.

Bagby, George W. *John Brown and William Mahone: An Historical Parallel Foreshadowing Civil Trouble.* Richmond, 1880.

Bartlett, William Francis. *Memoir of William Francis Bartlett.* Edited by Francis W. Palfrey. Boston: Houghton, Osgood, 1878.

"The Battle of the Crater." *Seminary,* November 1869, 93–102.

Bernard, George S., ed. *War Talks of Confederate Veterans.* Petersburg: Fen and Owen, 1892.

Bosbyshell, Oliver C. *The 48th in the War.* Philadelphia: Avil, 1895.

Bowley, Freeman S. "The Petersburg Mine." In *Papers Prepared and Read before the California Commandery of the Loyal Legion of the United States.* Wilmington: Broadfoot, 1995.

Carroll, Andrew, ed. *War Letters: Extraordinary Correspondence from American Wars.* New York: Scribner's, 2001.

Carter, Joseph C. *Magnolia Journey: A Union Veteran Revisits the Former Confederate States.* Tuscaloosa: University of Alabama Press, 1974.

• Chamberlain, Joshua Lawrence. *The Grand Old Man of Maine: Selected Letters of Joshua Lawrence Chamberlain, 1865–1914.* Edited by Jeremiah E. Goulka. Chapel Hill: University of North Carolina Press, 2004.

Chamberlayne, C. G. *Ham Chamberlayne—Virginian.* 1932. Reprint, Wilmington: Broadfoot, 1992.

Chambers, H. A. "The Bloody Crater." *Confederate Veteran* 31 (May 1923): 174–77.

———. *Diary of Captain Henry A. Chambers.* Edited by T. H. Pearce. Wendell, N.C.: Broadfoot's Bookmark, 1983.

Christian, George L. "North Carolina and Virginia in the Civil War." *Confederate Veteran* 12 (April 1904): 161–69.

The Civil War Centennial and the Negro: Slavery, Civil War. N.p.: Vanguard Society of America, 1961.

Clark, George. "Alabamians in the Crater Battle." *Confederate Veteran* 3 (February 1895): 68–69.

Day, W. A. "Battle of the Crater." *Confederate Veteran* 11 (August 1903): 355–56.

De Peyster, J. Watts. "A Military Memoir of William Mahone, a Major General in the Confederate Army." *New York Historical Magazine,* July 1870, 12–33.

Dickert, Augustus D. *History of Kershaw's Brigade.* Newberrry, S.C.: Elbert H. Aull, 1899.

Dodge, Theodore A. *A Bird's-Eye View of Our Civil War.* Cambridge, Mass.: Riverside, 1883.

Elliott, James C. *The Southern Soldier Boy: A Thousand Shots for the Confederacy.* Raleigh: Edwards and Broughton, 1907.

Embick, Milton A., ed. *Military History of the Third Division.* Harrisburg, Pa.: C. E. Aughinbaugh, 1913.

Evans, Robert G., ed. *The 16th Mississippi Infantry: Civil War Letters and Reminiscences.* Jackson: University Press of Mississippi, 2002.

Featherston, John C. *Battle of the Crater.* 1906. Reprint, Birmingham: Birmingham Public Library Press, 1987.

Flanner, Henry G. "Flanner's North Carolina Battery at the Battle of the Crater." *Southern Historical Society Papers* 5 (May 1878): 247–48.

"Gen. David A. Weisiger, of Virginia." *Confederate Veteran* 7 (August 1899): 362–64.

Gould, Joseph. *The Story of the Forty-eighth.* Philadelphia: Frank H. Taylor, 1908.

Holt, David. *A Mississippi Rebel in the Army of Northern Virginia: The Civil War Memoirs of Private David Holt.* Edited by Thomas D. Cockrell and Michael Ballard. Baton Rouge: Louisiana State University Press, 1995.

Humphreys, Andrew A. *The Virginia Campaign, 1864 and 1865.* 1883. Reprint, New York: Da Capo, 1995.

Johnson, Edward A. *A School History of the Negro Race in America from 1619 to 1890.* Raleigh: Edwards and Broughton, 1890.

Jones, R. W. "Mahone's Men at the Crater." *Confederate Veteran* 16 (January 1908): 3.

Kilmer, George L. "The Dash into the Crater." *Century,* September 1887, 774–76.

Kingsburg, T. B. "North Carolina at Gettysburg." *Our Living and Our Dead,* November 1874, 457–63.

Lane, James H. "The Truth of History." *Southern Historical Society Papers* 18 (January 1890): 72–80.

Mahoneism Unveiled! N.p., 1871.

McCabe, Gordon W. "Defense of Petersburg." *Southern Historical Society Papers* 6 (December 1876): 257–306.

McCallister, Robert. *The Civil War Letters of General Robert McCallister.* Edited by James I. Robertson. Baton Rouge: Louisiana State University Press, 1998.

McMaster, Fitz W. "The Battle of the Crater, July 30, 1864." *Southern Historical Society Papers* 10 (March 1882): 119–30.

Meyers, Terry, ed. "John Nichols Visit to Virginia, 1865: 'The James River.'" *Victorians Institute Journal* 30 (2002): 141–52.

Moseley, Ronald, ed. *The Stilwell Letters: A Georgian in Longstreet's Corps, Army of Northern Virginia.* Macon: Mercer University Press, 2002.

Petersburg National Battlefield: Educator's Guide, 2006–2007. Petersburg: Petersburg National Battlefield's Division of Interpretation, 2006. Available at PNB.

Petersburg National Battlefield: Final General Management Plan. Petersburg: National Park Service, 2004. Available at PNB.

Phillips, B. F. "Wilcox's Alabamians in Virginia." *Confederate Veteran* 15 (November 1907): 490.

Pollard, Edward A. *The Lost Cause.* 1866. Reprint, New York: Gramercy, 1994.

———. *Southern History of the War.* Vol 2. New York: Charles B. Richardson, 1866.

Rhodes, Elisha H. *All for the Union: The Civil War Diary and Letters of Elisha H. Rhodes.* Edited by Robert H. Rhodes. New York: Orion Books, 1985.

Rockwell, William L., ed. *Dear Frank: The War Years.* N.p., 2001.

Rogers, George T. "The Crater Battle, 30th July, 1864." *Confederate Veteran* 3 (January 1895): 12–14.

Shaver, Lewellyn A. *Gracie's Alabama Brigade.* Montgomery: Barrett and Brown, 1867.

Silliker, Ruth L., ed. *The Rebel Yell and the Yankee Hurrah: The Civil War Journal of a Maine Volunteer.* Camden, Maine: Down East Books, 1985.

Stewart, William H. "Crater Legion of Mahone's Brigade." *Confederate Veteran* 11 (December 1903): 557–58.

———. *Description of the Battle of the Crater.* Norfolk: Landmark Book and Job Office, 1876.

Taylor, Walter Herron. *Lee's Adjutant: The Wartime Letters of Colonel Walter Herron Taylor, 1862–1865.* Edited by R. Lockwood Tower. Columbia: University of South Carolina Press, 1995.

Thomas, Henry G. "The Colored Troops at Petersburg." *Century,* September 1887, 777–82.

Trowbridge, John T. *The Desolate South, 1865–66.* 1868. Reprint, Boston: Little, Brown, 1956.

Vance, P. M. "Incidents of the Crater Battle." *Confederate Veteran* 14 (April 1906): 178.

Voris, Alvin C. *A Citizen-Soldier's Civil War: The Letters of Brevet Major General Alvin C. Voris.* Edited by Jerome Mushkat. De Kalb: Northern Illinois University Press, 2002.

Watson, Keith, ed. *Honor in Command: Lt. Freeman S. Bowley's Civil War Services in the 30th United States Colored Infantry.* Gainesville: University Press of Florida, 2006.

Weld, Stephen W. *War Diary and Letters of Stephen M. Weld, 1861–1865.* 2nd ed. Boston: Massachusetts Historical Society, 1979.

Whitman, George Washington. *Civil War Letters of George Washington Whitman.* Edited by Jerome M. Loving. Durham: Duke University Press, 1975.

Wightman, Edward. "The Roughest Kind of Campaigning: Letters of Sergeant Edward Wightman, Third New York Volunteers, May–July 1864." Edited by Edward Longacre. *Civil War History* 28 (December 1982): 324–51.

Williams, D. B. *A Sketch of the Life and Times of Capt. R. A. Paul.* Richmond: Johns and Goolsby, 1885.

Williams, George W. *A History of the Negro Troops in the War of the Rebellion, 1861–1865.* New York: Harper and Brothers, Franklin Square, 1888.

Wise, John S. *The End of an Era.* Boston: Houghton Mifflin, 1899.

Secondary Works

Alexander, Ann F. *Race Man: The Rise and Fall of the "Fighting Editor," John Mitchell Jr.* Charlottesville: University Press of Virginia, 2003.

Anderson, Paul C. *Blood Image: Turner Ashby in the Civil War and the Southern Mind.* Baton Rouge: Louisiana State University Press, 2002.

Arsenault, Raymond. *Freedom Riders: 1961 and the Struggle for Racial Justice.* New York: Oxford University Press, 2006.

Ayers, Edward L. *Promise of the New South: Life After Reconstruction.* New York: Oxford University Press, 1992.

Ayers, Edward L., and John C. Willis, eds. *The Edge of the South: Life in Nineteenth Century Virginia.* Charlottesville: University Press of Virginia, 1991.

Blair, William. *Cities of the Dead: Contesting the Memory of the Civil War in the South, 1865–1914.* Chapel Hill: University of North Carolina Press, 2004.

Blake, Nelson M. *William Mahone of Virginia: Soldier and Political Insurgent.* Richmond: Garrett and Massie, 1935.

Blatt, Martin J., Thomas J. Brown, and Donald Yacovone, eds. *Hope and Glory: Essays on the Legacy of the 54th Massachusetts Regiment.* Amherst: University of Massachusetts Press, 2001.

Blight, David W. *Beyond the Battlefield: Race, Memory, and the American Civil War.* Amherst: University of Massachusetts Press, 2002.

———. *Race and Reunion: The Civil War in American Memory.* Cambridge, Mass.: Harvard University Press, 2001.

Bodnar, John. *Remaking America: Public Memory, Commemoration, and Patriotism in the Twentieth Century.* Princeton: Princeton University Press, 1992.

Branch, Taylor. *Parting the Waters: America in the King Years, 1954–63.* New York: Simon and Schuster, 1988.

Brown, Thomas J. "Civil War Remembrance as Reconstruction." In *Reconstructions: New Perspectives on the Postbellum United States,* 206–36. New York: Oxford University Press, 2006.

Brundage, W. Fitzhugh. *The Southern Past: A Clash of Race and Memory.* Cambridge, Mass.: Harvard University Press, 2005.

———, ed. *Where These Memories Grow: History, Memory, and Southern Identity.* Chapel Hill: University of North Carolina Press, 2000.

Cannan, John. *The Crater.* Cambridge, Mass.: Da Capo, 2002.

Carmichael, Peter S. *The Last Generation: Young Virginians in Peace, War, and Reunion.* Chapel Hill: University of North Carolina Press, 2005.

———. *Lee's Young Artillerist: William R. J. Pegram.* Charlottesville: University Press of Virginia, 1995.

Carter, Joseph C., ed. *Magnolia Journey: A Union Veteran Revisits the Former Confederate States.* Tuscaloosa: University of Alabama Press, 1974.

Cashin, Joan E., ed. *The War Was You and Me: Civilians in the American Civil War.* Princeton: Princeton University Press, 2002.

Cavanaugh, Michael A., and William Marvel. *The Battle of the Crater: "The Horrid Pit."* Lynchburg: H. E. Howard, 1989.

Cimprich, John. *Fort Pillow, a Civil War Massacre, and Public Memory.* Baton Rouge: Louisiana State University Press, 2006.

Clark, Kathleen Ann. *Defining Moments: African American Commemoration and Popular Culture in the South, 1863–1913.* Chapel Hill: University of North Carolina Press, 2005.

Cook, Robert J. *Troubled Commemoration: The American Civil War Centennial, 1961–1965.* Baton Rouge: Louisiana State University Press, 2007.

———. "(Un)Furl That Banner: The Response of White Southerners to the Civil War Centennial of 1961–1965." *Journal of Southern History,* November 2002, 879–912.

Cornish, Dudley T. *The Sable Arm: Black Troops in the Union Army, 1861–1865.* New York: Longmans, Green, 1956.

Coski, John M. *The Confederate Battle Flag: America's Most Embattled Emblem.* Cambridge, Mass.: Harvard University Press, 2005.

Cozzens, Peter, ed. *Battles and Leaders of the Civil War.* Vol. 6. Urbana: University of Illinois Press, 2004.

Cullen, Joseph P. "The Siege of Petersburg." *Civil War Times Illustrated,* August 1970, 4–17.

Cunningham, Roger D. "They Are as Proud of Their Uniform as Any Who Serve Virginia: African American Participation in the Virginia Volunteers, 1872–99." *Virginia Magazine of History and Biography* 110 (2002): 293–338.

Dabney, Virginius. *Virginia: The New Dominion.* Charlottesville: University Press of Virginia, 1971.

Dailey Jane. *Before Jim Crow: The Politics of Race in Postemancipation Virginia.* Chapel Hill: University of North Carolina Press, 2000.

———. "General William Mahone of Virginia: A Case of Historical Amnesia." Paper presented at the Douglas Southall Freeman and Southern Intellectual History Circle Conference, University of Richmond, February 21–24, 2002.

Dailey, Jane, Glenda E. Gilmore, and Bryant Simon, eds. *Jumpin' Jim Crow: Southern Politics from Civil War to Civil Rights.* Princeton: Princeton University Press, 2000.

Dean, Adam W. "'Who Controls the Past Controls the Future': The Virginia History Textbook Controversy." *Virginia Magazine of History and Biography* 117 (2009): 318–55.

Degler, Carl N. *The Other South: Southern Dissenters in the Nineteenth Century.* New York: Harper and Row, 1974.

Desjardin, Thomas A. *These Honored Dead: How the Story of Gettysburg Shaped American Memory.* Cambridge, Mass.: Da Capo, 2003.

Dickens, W. Jackson. "An Arm and a Leg for the Confederacy: Virginia's Disabled Veteran Legislation, 1865 to 1868." M.A. thesis, University of Richmond, 1997.

Dunkelman, Mark H. *Brothers One and All: Esprit de Corps in a Civil War Regiment.* Baton Rouge: Louisiana State University Press, 2004.

Eicher, David J. *The Longest Night: A Military History of the Civil War.* New York: Simon and Schuster, 2001.

Fabre, Genevieve, and Robert O'Meally, eds. *History and Memory in African-American Culture.* New York: Oxford University Press, 1994.

Fahs, Alice, and Joan Waugh, eds. *The Memory of the Civil War in American Culture.* Chapel Hill: University of North Carolina Press, 2004.

Foner, Eric. *Reconstruction: America's Unfinished Revolution, 1863–1877.* New York: Harper and Row, 1988.

Foster, Gaines M. *Ghosts of the Confederacy.* New York: Oxford University Press, 1987.

Franklin, John Hope. *George Washington Williams: A Biography.* Durham: Duke University Press, 1998.

Freeman, Douglas S. *Lee's Lieutenants: A Study in Command.* 4 vols. New York: Simon and Schuster, 1944.

———. *Robert E. Lee.* 4 vols. New York: Simon and Schuster, 1935.

French, Scot. *The Rebellious Slave: Nat Turner in American Memory.* Boston: Houghton Mifflin, 2004.

Gallagher, Gary W. *Jubal A. Early, the Lost Cause, and Civil War History: A Persistent Legacy.* Milwaukee: Marquette University Press, 1995.

———. *Lee and His Army in Confederate History.* Chapel Hill: University of North Carolina Press, 2001.

———. *Lee and His Generals in War and Memory.* Baton Rouge: Louisiana State University Press, 1998.

———. "Reevaluating Virginia's 'Shared History.'" *Civil War Times,* August 2010, 21–22.

———, ed. *The Spotsylvania Campaign.* Chapel Hill: University of North Carolina Press, 1998.

———, ed. *Three Days at Gettysburg: Essays on Confederate and Union Leadership.* Kent: Kent State University Press, 1999.

Gallagher, Gary W., and Alan Nolan, eds. *The Myth of the Lost Cause and Civil War History.* Bloomington: Indiana University Press, 2000.

Getz, Elizabeth A. "Looking to the Higher Ground: Historians at the Fredericksburg and Spotsylvania National Military Park Respond to FY-2000." M.A. thesis, University of North Carolina at Chapel Hill, 2003.

Glatthaar, Joseph T. *Forged in Battle: The Civil War Alliance of Black Soldiers and White Officers.* New York: Free Press, 1991.

Goldfield, David. *Southern Histories: Public, Personal, and Sacred.* Athens: University of Georgia Press, 2003.

———. *Still Fighting the Civil War: The American South and Southern History.* Baton Rouge: Louisiana State University Press, 2002.

Gordon, Lesley J. *General George E. Pickett in Life and Legend.* Chapel Hill: University of North Carolina Press, 1998.

Grant, Susan M., and Peter J. Parish, eds. *Legacy of Disunion: The Enduring Significance of the American Civil War.* Baton Rouge: Louisiana State University Press, 2003.

Greene, Wilson A. *Civil War Petersburg: Confederate City in the Crucible of War.* Charlottesville: University Press of Virginia, 2006.

Greenspan, Anders. *Creating Colonial Williamsburg.* Washington, D.C.: Smithsonian Institution Press, 2002.

Grimsley, Mark. *And Keep Moving On: The Virginia Campaign, May–June 1864.* Lincoln: University of Nebraska Press, 2002.

A Guide to the Fortifications and Battlefields around Petersburg. Reprint, N.p., Eastern National, 2003.

Hadden, Sally E. *Slave Patrols: Law and Violence in Virginia and the Carolinas.* Cambridge, Mass.: Harvard University Press, 2001.

Hahn, Steven. *A Nation under Our Feet: Black Political Struggles in the Rural South from Slavery to the Great Migration.* Cambridge, Mass.: Harvard University Press, 2003.

Happel, Ralph. "John A. Elder." *Commonwealth,* August 1937, 23–25.

Harrison, M. Clifford. *Home to the Cockade City: The Partial Biography of a Southern Town.* Richmond: Deitz, 1942.

Hassler, William W. "Scrappy Little 'Billy' Mahone." *Civil War Times Illustrated,* April 1963, 19–23.

Henderson, William D. *Gilded Age City: Politics, Life and Labor in Petersburg, Virginia, 1874–1889.* Lanham, Md.: University Press of America, 1980.

———. *Petersburg in the Civil War: War at the Door.* Lynchburg: H. E. Howard, 1998.

Hess, Earl J. *In the Trenches at Petersburg: Field Fortifications and Confederate Defeat.* Chapel Hill: University of North Carolina Press, 2009.

———. *Into the Crater: The Mine Attack at Petersburg.* Columbia: University of South Carolina Press, 2010.

Horton, James O., and Lois E. Horton, eds. *Slavery and Public History: The Tough Stuff of American Memory.* New York: New Press, 2006.

Johnson, David E. *Douglas Southall Freeman.* Gretna, La.: Pelican, 2002.

Johnston, James H. "The Participation of Negroes in the Government of Virginia from 1877 to 1888." *Journal of Negro History* 14 (1929): 251–71.

Kachun, Mitch. *Festivals of Freedom: Memory and Meaning in African American Emancipation Celebrations, 1808–1915.* Amherst: University of Massachusetts Press, 2003.

Kammen, Michael. *Mystic Chords of Memory: The Transformation of Tradition in American Culture.* New York: Random House, 1991.

Kaser, James A. *At the Bivouac of Memory: History, Politics and the Battle of Chickamauga.* New York: Peter Lang, 1996.

Krick, Robert E. L. *Staff Officers in Gray: A Biographical Register of the Staff Officers in the Army of Northern Virginia.* Chapel Hill: University of North Carolina Press, 2003.

Levin, Kevin M. "The Battle of the Crater, National Reunion, and the Creation of the Petersburg National Military Park, 1864–1937." *Virginia Social Science Journal* 41 (2006): 13–34.

———. "The Battle of the Crater, William Mahone, and Civil War Memory." M.A. thesis, University of Richmond, 2005.

———. "'Is Not the Glory Enough to Give Us All a Share?': An Analysis of Competing Memories of the Crater." In *The View from the Ground: Experiences of Civil War Soldiers,* edited by Aaron Sheehan-Dean, 227–48. Lexington: University of Kentucky Press, 2006.

———. "'On That Day You Consummated the Full Measure of Your Fame': Confederates Remember the Battle of the Crater." *Southern Historian* 25 (2004): 18–39.

———. "'Until Every Negro Has Been Slaughtered': Did Southerners See the Battle of the Crater as a Slave Rebellion?" *Civil War Times,* October 2010, 32–37.

———. "William Mahone, the Lost Cause, and Civil War History." *Virginia Magazine of History and Biography* 113 (2005): 378–412.

Levine, Bruce. *Confederate Emancipation: Southern Plans to Free and Arm Slaves during the Civil War.* New York: Oxford University Press, 2006.

Linderman, Gerald F. *Embattled Courage: The Experience of Combat in the American Civil War.* New York: Free Press, 1987.

Lindgren, James M. *Preserving the Old Dominion: Historic Preservation and Virginia Traditionalism.* Charlottesville: University Press of Virginia, 1993.

Manning Chandra. *What This Cruel War Was Over: Soldiers, Slavery, and the Civil War.* New York: Knopf, 2007.

Margalit, Avishai. *The Ethics of Memory.* Cambridge, Mass.: Harvard University Press, 2002.

Marvel, William. "And Fire Shall Devour Them: The 9th New Hampshire in the Crater." *Civil War Regiments* 2 (1992): 124–33.

———. *Burnside.* Chapel Hill: University of North Carolina Press, 1991.

Matter, William D. *If It Takes All Summer: The Battle of Spotsylvania.* Chapel Hill: University of North Carolina Press, 1998.

McConnell, Stuart. *Glorious Contentment: The Grand Army of the Republic, 1865–1900.* Chapel Hill: University of North Carolina Press, 1992.

McPherson, James M. *For Cause and Comrades: Why Men Fought in the Civil War.* New York: Oxford University Press, 1997.

McPherson, James M., and William J. Cooper, eds. *Writing the Civil War: The Quest to Understand.* Columbia: University of South Carolina Press, 1998.

McWhiney, Grady, and Jack J. Jenkins, eds. "The Union's Worst General." *Civil War Times Illustrated,* June 1995, 30–39.

Miller, Edward A., Jr. *The Black Civil War Soldiers of Illinois: The Story of the Twenty-ninth U.S. Colored Infantry.* Columbia: University of South Carolina Press, 1998.

Mitchell, Reid. *Civil War Soldiers.* New York: Viking Penguin, 1998.

Moger, Allen M. *Virginia: Bourbonism to Byrd, 1870–1925.* Charlottesville: University Press of Virginia, 1968.

Moore, James T. "Black Militancy in Readjuster Virginia, 1879–1883." *Journal of Southern History* 41 (May 1975): 167–86.

———. "The Death of the Duel: The Code Duello in Readjuster Virginia." *Virginia Magazine of History and Biography* 83 (1975): 259–76.

———. *Two Paths to the South: The Virginia Debt Controversy, 1870–1883.* Lexington: University of Kentucky Press, 1974.

Neff, John. *Honoring the Civil War Dead: Commemoration and the Problem of Reconciliation.* Lawrence: University Press of Kansas, 2005.

Nelson, Scott R. *Iron Confederacies: Southern Railways, Klan Violence, and Reconstruction.* Chapel Hill: University of North Carolina Press, 1999.

Noe, Kenneth W. "'Damned North Carolinians' and 'Brave Virginians': The Lane-Mahone Controversy, Honor, and Civil War Memory." *Journal of Military History* 72, no. 4 (2008): 1089–1116.

Oates, Stephen B. *The First of Jubilee: Nat Turner's Fierce Rebellion.* New York: Harper and Row, 1990.

Osborne, Charles C. *Jubal: The Life and Times of General Jubal A. Early, CSA, Defender of the Lost Cause.* Chapel Hill: Algonquin Books, 1992.

Parish, Peter J. *Slavery: History and Historians.* New York: Harper and Row, 1989.

Parramore, Thomas C., Peter C. Stewart, and Tommy L. Bogger. *Norfolk: The First Four Centuries.* Charlottesville: University Press of Virginia, 1994.

Piston, William G. *Lee's Tarnished Lieutenant: James Longstreet and His Place in Southern History.* Athens: University of Georgia Press, 1987.

Poole, W. Scott. *Never Surrender: Confederate Memory and Conservatism in the South Carolina Upcountry.* Athens: University of Georgia Press, 2004.

Power, J. Tracy. *Lee's Miserables*. Chapel Hill: University of North Carolina Press, 1998.

Pressly, Thomas J. *Americans Interpret Their Civil War*. New York: Free Press, 1962.

Pritched, William H., and Edgar A. Toppin. "The Relationship between Black Voting Power and Desegregation in Petersburg, Virginia from 1960 to 1974." M.A. thesis, Virginia State College, 1976.

Quarles, Benjamin. *The Negro in the Civil War*. Boston: Little, Brown, 1953.

Reardon, Carol. *Pickett's Charge in History and Memory*. Chapel Hill: University of North Carolina Press, 1997.

Robertson, James I., ed. "English Views of the Civil War: A Unique Excursion to Virginia, April 2–8, 1865." *Virginia Quarterly* 44 (Spring 1968): 201–12.

Rugemer, Edward B. *The Problem of Emancipation: The Caribbean Roots of the American Civil War*. Baton Rouge: Louisiana State University Press, 2008.

Rugh, Susan S. *Are We There Yet? The Golden Age of American Family Vacations*. Lawrence: University Press of Kansas, 2008.

Scott, James G., and Edward A. Wyatt, eds. *Petersburg's Story: A History*. Richmond: Deitz, 1960.

Shackel, Paul A. *Memory in Black and White: Race, Commemoration, and the Post-bellum Landscape*. New York: Altamira, 2003.

Shaffer, Donald R. *After the Glory: The Struggles of Black Civil War Veterans*. Lawrence: University Press of Kansas, 2004.

Silber, Nina. *The Romance of Reunion*. Chapel Hill: University of North Carolina Press, 1993.

Skoch, George, and Mark W. Perkins, eds. *Lone Star Confederate*. College Station: Texas A&M University Press, 2003.

Slotkin, Richard. *No Quarter: The Battle of the Crater, 1864*. New York: Random House, 2009.

Smith, J. Douglas. *Managing White Supremacy: Race, Politics, and Citizenship in Jim Crow Virginia*. Chapel Hill: University of North Carolina Press, 2002.

Smith, John D., ed. *Black Soldiers in Blue: African American Troops in the Civil War Era*. Chapel Hill: University of North Carolina Press, 2002.

Smith, Timothy B. *The Golden Age of Battlefield Preservation: The Decade of the 1890's and the Establishment of America's First Five Military Parks*. Knoxville: University of Tennessee Press, 2008.

———. *This Great Battlefield of Shiloh: History, Memory, and the Establishment of a Civil War National Military Park*. Knoxville: University of Tennessee Press, 2004.

Stephens, Travis J. L. "Participation of Negro Troops in 'the Battle of the Crater,' July 30, 1864." M.A. thesis, Virginia State College, 1967.

Stevens, Robert J. *Captain Bill*. Richburg, S.C.: Chester District Genealogical Society, 1985.

Stone, Dewitt B., Jr., ed. *Wandering to Glory: Confederate Veterans Remember Evans' Brigade.* Columbia: University of South Carolina Press, 2002.

Suderow, Bryce A. "The Battle of the Crater: The Civil War's Worst Massacre." *Civil War History* 43 (September 1997): 219–24.

———. "Confederate Casualties at the Crater." *Kepi* 3 (June–July 1985): 24–33.

———. "Glory Denied: The First Battle of Deep Bottom, July 27th–29th, 1864." *North and South,* September 2000, 17–32.

Sutton, Robert K., ed. *Rally on the High Ground: The National Park Service Symposium on the Civil War.* N.p., Eastern National, 2000.

Thelen, David. "Memory and American History." *Journal of American History* 75 (March 1989): 1117–29.

Toplin, Robert B., ed. *Ken Burns's* The Civil War: *Historians Respond.* New York: Oxford University Press, 1996.

Trask, Benjamin H. *61st Virginia Infantry.* Lynchburg: H. E. Howard, 1988.

Traxel, David. *1898: The Tumultuous Year of Victory, Invention, Internal Strife, and Industrial Expansion That Saw the Birth of the American Century.* New York: Knopf, 1998.

Trudeau, Noah A. *The Last Citadel.* Baton Rouge: Louisiana State University Press, 1991.

———. *Like Men of War: Black Troops in the Civil War.* New York: Little, Brown, 1998.

———. "A Stranger in the Club: The Army of the Potomac's Black Division." In *Slavery, Resistance, Freedom,* edited by Gabor Boritt and Scott Hancock, 96–102. New York: Oxford University Press, 2004.

Waldrep, Christopher. *Vicksburg's Long Shadow: The Civil War Legacy of Race and Remembrance.* Lanham, Md.: Rowan and Littlefield, 2005.

Wallenstein, Peter. *Blue Laws and Black Codes: Conflict, Courts, and Change in Twentieth-Century Virginia.* Charlottesville: University Press of Virginia, 2004.

Warner, Ezra J. *Generals in Blue: Lives of the Union Commanders.* Baton Rouge: Louisiana State University Press, 1964.

———. *Generals in Gray: Lives of the Confederate Commanders.* Baton Rouge: Louisiana State University Press, 1959.

Warren, Craig A. "'Oh God, What a Pity!': The Irish Brigade at Fredericksburg and the Creation of Myth." *Civil War History* 47 (September 2001): 193–222.

Waugh, John C. *Lincoln's Reelection: The Battle for the Presidency.* New York: Crown, 1997.

Weeks, Jim. *Gettysburg: Memory, Market, and an American Shrine.* Princeton: Princeton University Press, 2003.

Wert, Jeffrey D. *General James Longstreet: The Confederacy's Most Controversial Soldier.* New York: Simon and Schuster, 1993.

———. *The Sword of Lincoln: The Army of the Potomac.* New York: Simon and Schuster, 2005.

Williams, Oscar R., III. "The Civil Rights Movement in Richmond and Petersburg Virginia during 1960." M.A. thesis, Virginia State University, 1990.

Wilson, Charles R. *Baptized in Blood: The Religion of the Lost Cause, 1865–1920.* Athens: University of Georgia Press, 1980.

Woodward, C. V. *Origins of the New South, 1877–1913.* Baton Rouge: Louisiana State University Press, 1951.

Wyatt-Brown, Bertram. *The Shaping of Southern Culture: Honor, Grace, and War, 1760's–1880's.* Chapel Hill: University of North Carolina Press, 2001.

Zenzen, Joan M. *Battling for Manassas.* University Park: Pennsylvania State University Press, 1998.

INDEX

NEW DIRECTIONS IN SOUTHERN HISTORY

SERIES EDITORS
Michele Gillespie, *Wake Forest University*
William A. Link, *University of Florida*

Southern Farmers and Their Stories: Memory and Meaning in Oral History
Melissa Walker

Law and Society in the South: A History of North Carolina Court Cases
John W. Wertheimer